KANSAS CITY CHIEFS

LEGENDS

JEFF DETERS

Copyright © 2019
Jeff Deters
Kansas City
Chiefs
Legends
All rights reserved.

No part of this publication may be reproduced, distributed, or transmitted in any form or by any means, including photocopying, recording, or other electronic or mechanical methods, without the prior written permission of the publisher, except in the case of brief quotations embodied in critical reviews and certain other non-commercial uses permitted by copyright law.

Deters Publications

Printed in the United States of America
First Printing 2019
First Edition 2019

ISBN: 978-1-7332697-0-4 (print)
ISBN: 978-1-7332697-1-1 (e-book)

10 9 8 7 6 5 4 3 2 1

Cover design by Angie Alaya
Cover photo: Scott Winters/Icon Sportswire
Back cover photo: Kenneth Spencer Research Library, University of Kansas Libraries

Table of Contents

INTRODUCTION..*i*

CHAPTER 1 1

  2019 AFC PLAYOFFS

    Bucking History 1

    Super Close 4

CHAPTER 2 7

  THE OWNERS

    Lamar Hunt 7

    Clark Hunt 17

CHAPTER 3 22

  GENERAL MANAGERS

    Jack Steadman 22

    Carl Peterson 27

    John Dorsey 31

    Brett Veach 34

CHAPTER 4 37

  THE COACHES

    Hank Stram 37

    Marty Schottenheimer 46

    Gunther Cunningham 57

    Dick Vermeil 62

    Andy Reid 65

CHAPTER 5 .... **73**
   QUARTERBACKS
      Len Dawson 73
      Joe Montana 81
      Trent Green 90
      Alex Smith 93
      Patrick Mahomes 97

CHAPTER 6 .... **106**
   RUNNING BACKS
      Mack Lee Hill 106
      Joe Delaney 108
      Christian Okoye 110
      Marcus Allen 116
      Priest Holmes 119
      Jamaal Charles 123

CHAPTER 7 .... **129**
   FULLBACK
      Tony Richardson 129

CHAPTER 8 .... **131**
   WIDE RECEIVERS
      Otis Taylor 131
      Tyreek Hill 136

CHAPTER 9 .... **140**
   TIGHT ENDS

    Tony Gonzalez 140

    Travis Kelce 145

CHAPTER 10 151
OFFENSIVE LINE

    Ed Budde 151

    Jack Rudnay 153

    John Alt 155

    Will Shields 157

    Brian Waters 160

    Willie Roaf 162

CHAPTER 11 164
DEFENSIVE LINE

    Buck Buchanan 164

    Curley Culp 167

    Neil Smith 169

    Chris Jones 172

CHAPTER 12 177
LINEBACKERS

    Bobby Bell 177

    Willie Lanier 181

    Derrick Thomas 185

    Tamba Hali 194

    Derrick Johnson 199

    Justin Houston 204

CHAPTER 13 208
DEFENSIVE BACKS
Johnny Robinson 208

Emmitt Thomas 210

Lloyd Burruss 212

Deron Cherry 215

Albert Lewis 219

Kevin Ross 223

Eric Berry 225

CHAPTER 14 231
SPECIAL TEAMS
Jan Stenerud 231

Nick Lowery 237

Dante Hall 245

Dustin Colquitt 247

Harrison Butker 253

CHAPTER 15 257
LEGENDS IN THE MAKING
The Class of 2019 257

CHAPTER 16 260
HOME OF THE CHIEFS
Arrowhead Stadium 260

ABOUT THE AUTHOR 263
BIBLIOGRAPHY 264

INTRODUCTION

NFL football isn't just on Sundays in the fall anymore. It's a way of life for many fans. In the last decade or so the league has done a great job making the sport a year-round event, and perhaps there is no better example than the Kansas City Chiefs.

The Chiefs have been in the hearts and minds of many since Lamar Hunt founded the team, first as the Dallas Texans then as the Chiefs when they moved to Kansas City in 1963. As the franchise begins its 60th season there is no shortage of Chiefs news, especially in this 24/7 news cycle we now live in, and every Chiefs fan is dreaming of a Super Bowl this season.

It's been 50 years since that magical 1969 season that culminated with a win in Super Bowl IV. To win a championship, you have to have great players and great coaches. The Chiefs had that back then with Len Dawson and Hank Stram and they have it now with NFL MVP Patrick Mahomes and Andy Reid.

They are just a few of the legends you will read about in the pages of this book. Though this book is confined to the owners, general managers, coaches and players, there are countless others who have contributed in some way to making the Chiefs one of the most successful and popular franchises in professional sports. From stadium employees to the media relations department to their fans across the world, all have given so much time and effort on behalf of the Chiefs organization.

Beginning as a young fan whose first memories of the Chiefs involved Marty Schottenheimer, Derrick Thomas and a lot of Tecmo Super Bowl, and later as a reporter, I have seen and covered a lot of great Chiefs games. But the best part of the Chiefs is the people.

Talking to so many current and former players for this book and hearing their stories was such a wonderful experience for me, and I hope you find reading about them to be equally enjoyable.

CHAPTER 1
2019 AFC PLAYOFFS

Bucking History

The Kansas City Chiefs have experienced almost everything there is to see at Arrowhead Stadium. Over the years, they've endured floods, sleet, ice, snow and especially long droughts.

Twenty-five years is a long time. That's how long it had been since the Chiefs last won a playoff game at home when they took the field on Jan. 12, 2019, to play their longtime nemesis the Indianapolis Colts.

Coming into the game, the Chiefs were 0-4 against the Colts all-time in the playoffs. In 1996, their kicker missed three field goals on an Arrowhead playing surface that looked more like an ice-skating rink than a football field. And in 2004, their defense couldn't force the visiting Colts to punt.

The road losses also were heartbreaking. In 2007, the Chiefs didn't get a first down in the first half. In 2014, they blew a 28-point second-half lead. So on another snowy day in Kansas City, the two teams converged again. This time the forces of nature were different. This time the Chiefs had Patrick Mahomes.

In his postseason debut, the NFL MVP sent the crowd home happy as the Chiefs won 31-13. Finally Chiefs fans could breathe a sigh of relief.

"It's huge," Mahomes said of the much-needed win. "These fans, we feed off the energy that they bring every single week. They are so intense. It really is surreal and crazy. You feel it the moment you step in the stadium, and it's an honor that we get to play in front of these fans."

Kansas City Chiefs quarterback Patrick Mahomes (15) dives for the pylon on a 4-yard touchdown run during the second quarter of the AFC Divisional Round playoff game against the Indianapolis on Jan.12, 2019, at Arrowhead Stadium in Kansas City, Mo. The Chiefs won 31-13, marking the team's first playoff win at home since January 1994. (Scott Winters/Icon Sportswire)

Mahomes connected on 27 of 41 passes for 278 yards and was in complete control despite having never played a game in the snow.

"I've played games where it's snowed before the game, or like with sleet and rain, but never snow," said Mahomes, a Texas native. "I actually thought it was pretty cool. The wind wasn't blowing that hard, so I felt like I could throw the ball pretty well still. And it was all about receivers keeping their feet underneath them and making the catches in the snow.

"I felt good in pregame warmups. We went out there to throw with the tarp off and felt like I was spinning it well."

Mahomes didn't throw a touchdown pass, but he ran for a score in the third quarter and helped push a teammate over the goal line for another score in the fourth quarter. Damien Williams rushed for 129 yards on 25 carries and scored the game's first touchdown, and Tyreek Hill soon followed with a 36-yard burst to put the Chiefs up 14-0.

The Chiefs defense played its best game of the season, sacking Andrew Luck three times and limiting him to just 203 yards passing.

"We wanted to light up the city," said defensive lineman Chris Jones. "We didn't want to take the road back down memory lane—first playoff game and we're out. We wanted to light up the city with fireworks and we wanted to keep going. I told them to get used to this feeling."

Emotions inside the Chiefs locker room are often a wide variety, ranging from elation to devastation. Before their win against the Colts, the Chiefs had lost 11 of their last 12 playoff games.

"I don't get caught up in any of that," Chiefs coach Andy Reid said. "I'm into history. I love history if it makes you better, you learn from it and you move forward. That was the important thing for our guys.

"Don't get caught up on all the stuff that happened in the past, but if there's something that you can learn from it—if it was the play before or the game before—let's make you even greater than you already are. You are one of 32 (teams) in the National Football League, just help make yourself better. That's the approach we went with."

The win also was a historic one for the Chiefs. For the first time in team history, they would now get to play for the Lamar Hunt Trophy at home.

"It's very special obviously for our family," said Chiefs owner Clark Hunt. "It's one of the goals that I always put for the players at the beginning of the year. The first thing we want to do is win the Lamar Hunt Trophy, then we want to go to the Super Bowl and win that Lombardi Trophy.

"We're excited to be able to do it at Arrowhead and be able to play for the championship in front of our great fans."

Super Close

As the trophy bearing his father's name was being presented to Tom Brady and the New England Patriots, just down the hall inside a somber Chiefs locker room, Clark Hunt shook hands and thanked his players for an amazing season.

Just a few minutes earlier the Chiefs' season came to an end with a 37-31 loss in overtime. Since 1984 the AFC champion has brought home the Lamar Hunt Trophy, aptly named for the man who founded the AFL and the Chiefs franchise. Until earlier that week, the trophy had never been inside Arrowhead Stadium.

Yet there it was, finally within reach for the Hunt family and the Chiefs, who led with two minutes to play in regulation after being down 14-0 at the half and 17-7 to start the fourth quarter. Hunt began the evening by leading the drum ceremony right before kickoff as 77,034 fans performed the Tomahawk Chop. After the game, the "super wolf blood moon" was supposed to be visible to Kansas City stargazers with its red-like hue commemorating a Chiefs win.

But late in regulation an offsides penalty on Dee Ford, and the flip of the coin to start overtime took the trophy away from Chiefs Kingdom.

"We try to make this a community effort and came up a little short," said Chiefs coach Andy Reid, who rarely shows emotion at the podium but did so after the tough loss. "But hopefully this gives us a little bit of what we have looking forward to us in the future, and that's where we'll go after we're done aching here.

"It's a bright future. We've got good players and we'll get over the hump here, the big hump. And that's this game right here."

The game itself made for great theater as Brady (30 of 46, 348 yards, 1 TD, 2 INTs) and Patrick Mahomes (16 of 31, 295 yards, 3 TDs) played for a spot in the Super Bowl. Nearly 54 million people watched the CBS broadcast, which was the highest-rated program on TV since Super Bowl LII.

The Chiefs had the game won, but on a crucial third-and-10 from the Chiefs' 34-yard line Brady threw a pass that tipped off the fingers of tight end Rob Gronkowski and landed in the waiting arms of defensive back Charvarius Ward. The Chiefs would have had the ball with 54 seconds to go in the fourth quarter and a four-point lead, but Ford was lined up in the neutral zone, and the Patriots kept the ball. Two plays later, Rex Burkhead scored the go-ahead touchdown, and later the game-winner in overtime.

"We've got to be better, me especially on that play," Ford said. "I've got to see the ball. I've got to see the ball, especially that time of the game and what was at stake."

Patrick Mahomes (15) threw three touchdown passes against Patrick Chung (23) and the New England Patriots in the AFC championship game on Jan. 20, 2019, at Arrowhead Stadium, but the Chiefs lost 37-31 in overtime. It was the Chiefs' first appearance in the AFC title game in 25 years. (Scott Winters/Icon Sportswire)

Mahomes, though, didn't blink. He quickly drove the Chiefs 48 yards to put the team in field-goal range, and Harrison Butker's 39-yarder sent it to overtime. But Mahomes never touched the ball again as the Patriots won the coin toss and advanced to the Super Bowl with a 13-play, 75-yard scoring drive.

The abrupt ending, though, even in its finality, marks a new era for the Chiefs. The 2018 season, the win against the Colts, and even the loss to the Patriots serves as a reminder that a dynasty of their own may be ahead, thanks to Mahomes and Co.

"Right now it's the end," Mahomes said. "But hopefully it's just the beginning of a long time."

CHAPTER 2
THE OWNERS

Lamar Hunt

We hear it so many times, to chase your dream. Doing so requires great courage, determination, vision and perseverance.

For Lamar Hunt, his dream was to own an NFL football team. And from the day he was born until the day he died, Hunt showed everyone what those qualities are all about.

A modest and bold man, Hunt originally hoped to one day own the NFL's Chicago Cardinals. But after years of rejection, he ultimately became founder of the American Football League, the Dallas Texans and the Kansas City Chiefs. Along with coach Hank Stram, Hunt made a point to scour the smaller black colleges for players as he felt they were being overlooked by the NFL in the early 1960s.

Even with an infusion of new talent, Hunt's new league was frowned upon for years by the well-established NFL. Still, it was Hunt who brought the merger of the two leagues together, coined the phrase "the Super Bowl" and transformed football into the game we know today.

A league of his own

The son of Texas oilman H.L. Hunt and Lyda Bunker Hunt, Lamar was born Aug. 2, 1932, in Eldorado, Ark. The youngest of seven children, his love for sports earned him the nickname "Games" by his siblings as he was always bouncing a ball or inventing some sort of contest.

Hunt grew up in Dallas and attended boarding school at the Hill School in Pottstown, Pa. He played quarterback and served as team captain his senior year. Hunt majored in geology at Southern Methodist University and was a third-string wide receiver on the football team from 1952-55.

After his playing days were done, Hunt enjoyed going to the local high school football games on Friday night then watching his alma mater play on Saturday. Hunt even traveled to all the SMU road games. But come Sunday, he would be at home glued to the TV watching the NFL.

In those days, Hunt was running a batting cage business and still working for the family business at Hunt Oil, which at one time was worth about $8 billion. Hunt, though, wanted to carve his own niche in the business world so he pondered what he enjoyed doing most. The answer was talking about sports and going to sporting events. So along those lines, he debated whether to buy a pro baseball team or football team.

Eventually Hunt decided on football, partly because he was fascinated by watching the 1958 NFL championship game between the Baltimore Colts and New York Giants on TV. It was the first NFL game to go to sudden death, and the Colts won 23-17 in what has since been called "the greatest game ever played."

Dallas didn't have a team then, but the young Hunt thought he could change that. Earlier that summer, he picked up the phone and dialed the NFL offices and commissioner Bert Bell answered. Hunt asked him if there was any chance the NFL would expand soon. Bell told him that was highly unlikely, but if he wanted to buy a team, he should contact the Walter Wolfner family, owners of the Chicago Cardinals.

The Cardinals had fallen on hard times having posted just one winning season in eight years. They were also competing with the Chicago Bears at the gate. Hunt's initial meeting with the Wolfners left him no closer to owning a football team, and subsequent meetings yielded similar results.

Lamar Hunt founded the American Football League and the Dallas Texans/Kansas City Chiefs franchise. He also coined the phrase "Super Bowl" and was inducted into the Pro Football Hall of Fame in 1972. (Cliff Welch/Icon Sportswire)

After a final meeting in Miami in February 1959, Hunt boarded an American Airlines plane to return to Dallas. In the four-hour flight due to weather conditions, Hunt had plenty of time to think. His mind drifted back to a question Wolfner had asked him earlier that day.

Wolfner wondered if Hunt knew any of the other potential buyers he was talking to, including a Houston oilman named K.S. "Bud" Adams. Hunt didn't know any of the interested parties, but the concept of forming a new football league took root.

"Why wouldn't a second league work?" Hunt thought. "There was an American and National League in baseball, why not football?"

Hunt asked the stewardess for some stationary to write on and he outlined a set of rules and regulations for his new league that included 15-game seasons and home teams getting 60 percent of the gate with road teams getting 40 percent.

Adams quickly signed up for Hunt's new league. With a business partner on board, Hunt hoped he could convince Bell to commission both leagues. Bell told him he couldn't do that, however, and on July28, Bell appeared before a Senate committee to notify them of the pending formation of a new rival league.

A couple weeks after Bell's appearance before the Senate, Hunt publicly announced that he would be starting his new league and Dallas and Houston would be awarded the first two teams. A couple weeks later, Hunt announced the league would be known as the American Football League and the cities of Denver, Los Angeles, New York, Minneapolis, Buffalo and Boston also would field teams.

Minneapolis, however, later backed out to accept an invitation to the NFL and Oakland took its place, becoming the eighth original member of the AFL. Entry fee into the league for each owner was $25,000 and a $100,000 performance bond. The eight owners would later be known as "The Foolish Club" due to huge financial losses their first couple years in business.

Going to Kansas City

After Hunt announced the formation of his new league, the NFL quickly went into expansion mode. The first city on the list was Dallas followed by Houston. A coincidence? Hardly.

NFL expansion wasn't supposed to take place until the 1961 season. But by the fall of 1960—the same year Hunt's Texans took the field—the Cowboys were also playing football in Dallas with the sole purpose of driving Hunt's team out of town.

The Cowboys went 0-11-1 that season while the Texans went 8-6. In the next two years, the Cowboys won a combined nine games.

In 1962, the Texans, armed with new quarterback Len Dawson, won the AFL title with a double-overtime win over the Houston Oilers, the two-time defending AFL champs. A winning football team, though, wasn't nearly enough to make ends meet.

When Hunt's father was told that his son lost a $1 million in the league's first year of existence, he said at that rate he would go broke in 150 years.

Still, the team also lost money the next two years so Hunt made the decision to pull up stakes and move the franchise to Kansas City before the start of the 1963 season.

In the fall of 1962, Kansas City Mayor H. Roe Bartle heard that Hunt was looking for a new home for his football team so he flew to Dallas to meet him. Bartle was a loud and ambitious man who weighed about 300 pounds, while the mild-mannered Hunt might have weighed half that.

The meeting went well, and Bartle invited Hunt to come to Kansas City for a tour. Hunt accepted the offer with one condition. He wanted Bartle to ensure the visit would be made in complete secrecy as he didn't want anyone in Dallas or Kansas City to know that he was seriously contemplating moving his team north, especially while the season was still going.

When Hunt arrived in Kansas City, the first place he went was old Municipal Stadium, home of the Athletics. The A's were the town's Major League Baseball team but by name only. They didn't have a winning record in the 13 seasons they were there.

Not wanting anyone at the stadium to recognize Hunt during his visit, Bartle introduced him as "Mr. Lamar." After spending a day with Bartle mapping out potential locations for a football team, Hunt returned to Dallas intrigued by the possibilities in Kansas City.

On Feb. 8, 1963, Hunt announced he would move his team to the Midwest if 25,000 season tickets could be sold in Kansas City. In the days and weeks that followed, he and Stram went to Kansas City and gave several speeches trying to boost ticket sales. Though they had only reached about half their goal, Hunt officially moved his franchise to Kansas City on May 22. Four days later he renamed it the "Chiefs."

Super Chiefs

In 1964, the AFL signed a five-year, $36 million contract with NBC to broadcast its games on TV. The agreement got the attention of NFL owners, and by the spring of 1966, they were becoming increasingly concerned about their declining profits.

The core of the problem was the "Mickey Mouse League," the name the NFL bestowed upon the AFL during its 10 seasons of existence for being what it considered an inferior brand of football. As competition to sign players kept driving up costs for both leagues, a merger between the two made a lot of sense. For months, Hunt and Cowboys general manager Tex Schramm negotiated a deal behind the scenes, and finally a press conference announcing the merger was held on June 8 in New York.

Among the points agreed upon in the merger, which took four more years to fully integrate, included that the league would be called the NFL, Pete Rozelle would stay on as commissioner, there would be one common draft and a championship game would be played between the two conference winners at the conclusion of the 1966 season and going forward.

At the press conference announcing the deal, Hunt was asked whether the AFL or NFL won the "war." Hunt didn't look at it that way at all.

"I think it's beneficial to both, frankly, and very beneficial to the fans all around the country," Hunt said of the merger. "I don't want to sound corny on that, but when you look at all the aspects of the championship game, personally I think it'll be one of the biggest sporting events of the year, every year in America."

The original name for the championship game was the "AFL-NFL World Championship Game," but that was considered too wordy and not easy to publicize. So Hunt suggested calling it the "Super Bowl." The name itself was inspired by a combination of the Super Ball—a magnificent bouncy ball his kids loved to play with around the house—and the Cotton Bowl, one of the bowl games he regularly attended. Hunt also suggested using Roman numerals for each game instead of traditional digits.

In 1966, Hunt's Chiefs went 11-2-1 in the regular season and beat the Bills in the AFL championship game to advance to the first Super Bowl against Vince Lombardi and the Green Bay Packers. The game was played Jan. 15, 1967, at the Coliseum in Los Angeles. It's hard to fathom today, but it wasn't a sellout. About a third of the seats were empty.

The Chiefs, of the so-called Mickey Mouse league, did not appreciate the lack of respect by the NFL. So prior to kickoff, Stram sent a team official to Disneyland to buy a bunch of Mickey Mouse beanies and he had the Chiefs trainer and a few other staff members wear them in the locker room before the game.

The Chiefs were 14-point underdogs, but trailed just 14-10 at halftime. In the locker room, Dawson smoked a cigarette and drank a Fresca as the team went over plans for the second half. But in the final 30 minutes, the Packers took control and won 35-10.

After the game, Lombardi was asked how the Chiefs compared to other teams in the NFL. The Hall of Fame coach was not impressed with Kansas City's squad.

"It doesn't compare with the National Football League's teams," Lombardi said. "That's what you want me to say, I said it. It doesn't rate with the top teams in our division."

Stram eventually heard about Lombardi's postgame comments and he was taken aback. Soon, though, the Chiefs would have everyone's respect by winning Super Bowl IV with a 23-7 rout over the Vikings.

Inside the winning locker room, Hunt admired the trophy and what he and his franchise had accomplished in a relatively short amount of time.

"It's pretty fantastic," Hunt said. "It's a beautiful trophy and it really is a satisfying conclusion to the 10 years of the American Football League."

Honoring the Founder

In 1972, Hunt was inducted into the Pro Football Hall of Fame and he hadn't even turned 40 yet. It was a just reward, though, as he helped bring pro football to other cities across the U.S. and he had put his own franchise in the Super Bowl twice.

Hunt's love for sports didn't end with football. He enjoyed basketball and was an original owner of the Chicago Bulls. Hunt also loved tennis and soccer. He founded World Championship Tennis in the late '60s, a time when the top players could not play professionally. He also founded the Kansas City Wizards soccer team, now known as Sporting Kansas City, and owned several MLS teams at one time or another. The U.S. Open Cup trophy also has his name on it, but it's as founder of the Chiefs and the AFL that he's known best.

"Lamar Hunt was special," Chiefs coach Andy Reid said. "He was special to the National Football League."

Reid's players also are well versed on Hunt and his legacy, and that includes quarterback Patrick Mahomes.

"I think an awesome thing that we do here with the player development team is that they take us through the whole history," Mahomes said. "We come over to the museum that we have at the stadium, they take us through how he made the AFL pretty much from scratch, and how he had this vision and made the AFL, which is now the AFC, and kind of combined it with the NFL, and made this beautiful league.

"And it truly is special to have someone like that who created your franchise. And you want to do whatever you can to bring honor to him and that family as they've helped make us a place where we can play and have fun and love the sport that we play."

At the Founder's Plaza at Arrowhead Stadium, there is a larger-than-life bronze statue dedicated to Hunt. With his sleeves rolled up, and wearing his trademark glasses, the statue looks to the north, much like he did when he moved his football franchise to Kansas City.

In the background there are eight fountains, each representing one of the original AFL teams. The Plaza's shape is based on the Vince Lombardi Trophy, and Hunt's influence on the Super Bowl. Hunt, of course, named the game and later renamed the championship trophy to honor Lombardi, who died in 1970.

These are just a few of the many ways the Chiefs honor Hunt, who died Dec. 13, 2006, in a Dallas hospital after an eight-year battle with prostate cancer.

"Given his humble nature, my father would never have let us go to so much trouble on his behalf," said his son, Clark, who as chairman has run the team since his father's passing. "From the start, it was clear that we had to have a space devoted to Lamar, and it had to be available to all fans."

One of Hunt's favorite things was walking through the parking lot and shaking hands and taking pictures with tailgaters at the stadium he loved so much. An innovator and founder, Hunt always saw himself in a different light. Even when he was living out his dream, he saw himself as one of them.

"He was a fan first," Clark said.

Clark Hunt

Too young to remember Super Bowl IV, Chiefs chairman Clark Hunt is hoping Super Bowl LIV is something he'll never forget.

On Feb. 2, 2020, the 54th Super Bowl will be played in Miami, marking the 50th anniversary of the Chiefs' first and so far only world championship. But after taking a big step forward last year, there is reason to believe this season will finally be the one where the Lamar Hunt and Vince Lombardi trophies return to Kansas City.

The biggest reason for optimism in 2019 and beyond is Patrick Mahomes, the franchise quarterback the team had been searching for since Len Dawson.

Chiefs owner Clark Hunt smiles before the start of a preseason game against the San Francisco 49ers on Aug. 11, 2017, at Arrowhead Stadium in Kansas City, Mo. Hunt has presided over the team since his father's death in 2006. (Scott Winters/Icon Sportswire)

"It's been very, very exciting for me and our entire family to watch Patrick play," said Hunt, who usually wears a smile, a suit and a Chiefs lapel pin. "Hopefully we're in the first minutes of the first quarter of a very long game where we're going to get to see Patrick play a lot of games in Kansas City. And ultimately the narrative on what kind of a player he is and where his standing is in the history of the Chiefs and the National Football League, that's going to be down the road where we'll learn all that.

"But as a start, you couldn't have asked for a better start. He is the type of quarterback that can create an opportunity for your team to compete for a championship every year. That's something we aspire to here in Kansas City, and having a young quarterback that we drafted that puts the franchise in this position, that's a huge plus."

To get Mahomes in red and gold, Hunt had to sign off on the draft-day trade in 2017. Moving up 17 spots and giving up a first-round pick is a steep price, but one that Hunt gladly agreed to pay at the insistence of Brett Veach, Andy Reid and John Dorsey.

"Brett did a tremendous job on scouting Patrick, and first getting Andy, and later John Dorsey," Hunt said. "It was an organizational decision to draft him. I don't want to minimize that, but Brett deserves a lot of credit.

"I probably heard about the interest a couple months before the draft. As we went through the preparation process there was a point where I sat down and watched a handful of plays with John so he could show me things that they were describing that he did at Texas Tech and that led to an organizational decision."

Rising son

Hunt was born on Feb. 19, 1965, in Dallas and graduated from St. Mark's School of Texas in 1983. He later married Tavia Shackles, a former Miss Kansas winner. When Clark was just 7, he was playing outside and a 300-pound urn fell on his right foot, pinning him to the ground.

His mangled foot required 75 stitches and surgery. He also was in a wheelchair for months. Hunt, though, eventually recovered and played football and soccer in high school and was a captain on the soccer team at Southern Methodist University.

Hunt also starred in the classroom. He majored in business administration with a concentration in finance and was an academic All-American. Twice he earned the school's highest academic honor, the Provost Award for Outstanding Scholar.

After graduating in 1987, he worked as an investment banker at Goldman Sachs for a couple years before returning home to work for his father on a variety of businesses, including the Chiefs. As a young man, Clark would often walk the parking lots with his father and meet fans before the game, a tradition he has continued.

After Lamar's death, the family's sports holdings were split equally among his four children, Lamar Jr., Sharron, Clark and Dan. Hunt's mother, Norma, also owns a small share.

Like his father, Clark keeps a rather low profile, especially compared to other owners in professional sports. Yet he holds considerable influence among them as a leading and trusted voice. In 2011, Hunt was one of a handful of owners that NFL commissioner Roger Goodell asked to negotiate the league's collective bargaining agreement.

Hunt also has served as chairman of the international committee for years. And in February, he was named chairman of the NFL's finance committee.

Hunt also is mindful of making the fan experience at Arrowhead Stadium top notch. In 2013, the Chiefs implemented stadium-wide Wi-Fi and introduced their mobile app. Continuous advances in technology have forced the Chiefs and the NFL to continue to work to put butts in the seats, but the Chiefs were sixth in the NFL in attendance in 2018 and their TV ratings were through the roof.

"It's been a lot of fun for me, and I think everybody who's a Chiefs fan to see all the interest in the Chiefs," Hunt said. "And that's a credit to the success we've had and that interest is not only here locally but nationally. It seems that everybody who went to Texas Tech is a Chiefs fan and that's great.

"Our local ratings are also higher than they've been in many, many years—and our local ratings have always been pretty good. But Andy, Patrick and the offense and the victories we're getting has taken that to a higher level."

Best foot forward

Just like his father, Clark is an avid soccer fan. He is owner of FC Dallas and previously owned Columbus Crew SC. Hunt also regularly attends the World Cup and is hopeful Kansas City could serve as a host, possibly in 2026. Arrowhead Stadium is on a short list of contending sites in the U.S. and a quarterfinal match is a definite possibility.

For years, FC Dallas has worn a patch with the initials L.H. on its jersey to honor Lamar's legacy. And in 2007, Clark requested that the NFL allow the Chiefs to wear a patch honoring their founder. The patch featuring the AFL logo with the letters L.H. at the bottom has since become part of the team's uniform. It is positioned prominently and purposely on the left chest where the logo will always be over the heart of every Chiefs player.

Clark will always be compared to his father, but their operating styles are different in many ways. Clark is indeed around the team more than Lamar was and he is far more aggressive at making changes.

In his first few years in charge, Hunt let go several longtime Chiefs employees, including general manager Carl Peterson in 2008. The early returns on Hunt's tenure were not good. The Chiefs went 10-38 in his first three seasons and had losing records in five of his first six years at the helm.

By the time Hunt hired Reid in January 2013, the organization had already gone through three other head coaches—Herm Edwards, Todd Haley and Romeo Crennel—and two GMs in Peterson and Scott Pioli.

After Hunt fired Pioli following the 2012 season he revised the organization's power structure. For the first time in team history the coach and general manager would both report directly to him, a wise move by Hunt designed to make sure the conflict that arose between Haley and Pioli wouldn't happen again on his watch. That largely worked, though, Hunt is now on his fourth GM after Dorsey was let go in the summer of 2017 and replaced by Veach.

Now just two years later, the organization is the strongest it has been since the 1990s. The Chiefs have won the last three AFC West titles and could be on the brink of accomplishing something the fans haven't seen in 50 years.

CHAPTER 3
GENERAL MANAGERS

Jack Steadman

For nearly 50 years, Jack Steadman served as Lamar Hunt's right-hand man. Whether it was on the sidelines or in the boardroom, where there was one, there was usually the other.

However, there was one area where initially the two were about as far apart as you could get. When Hunt decided to move his football team from Dallas to Kansas City, he wanted the team name to go with it. That's right, the Kansas City Texans is what Hunt originally wanted to call his new team in Missouri.

Coach Hank Stram also was in favor of keeping the name the same, but Steadman, the team's general manager, believed doing so would prove disastrous.

"This isn't going to work," Steadman told Hunt.

Steadman got Hunt to reconsider and a name the team contest drew over 4,000 submissions. The most popular entries were the Mules, Royals and Stars. But on May 26, 1963, Hunt chose to call his team the Chiefs.

Despite it totaling only 42 votes in the contest, the name Chiefs appealed to Hunt for a couple reasons. For starters, it would honor the long Native American history of the area, and it would honor Kansas City Mayor H. Roe Bartle, who played a large role in bringing the team to town. Bartle also just happened to have the nickname "Chief," which he earned from his years as a Boy Scout.

A few months prior to the announcement of the team name, in January 1963, Steadman accompanied Hunt to Kansas City on a covert mission of sorts. They were still trying to gauge how Kansas City might welcome a pro football team while trying to maintain anonymity.

Hunt had already been there once before to meet with Roe, but Steadman had not. So he needed something to shroud his presence.

Jack X

The Muehlebach Hotel located in downtown Kansas City opened in 1915 and served as host for every President from Theodore Roosevelt to Ronald Reagan. Missouri's own Harry Truman was such a frequent guest that the hotel became known as "White House West."

Among the hotel's other famous patrons were Babe Ruth, Elvis Presley and the Beatles. Hunt and Steadman also stayed there, but around town Bartle introduced Steadman as "Jack X," a man he said was in town doing some investigative work. Rumors began to swirl that this mysterious "Jack X" worked for the FBI, but in truth he only worked for Hunt.

Steadman was born on Sept. 14, 1928, in Warrenville, Ill., and grew up in Dallas. He was an offensive and defensive lineman in high school and attended Baylor before graduating from SMU with a business degree.

Fresh out of college, Steadman got a job as an accountant for Hunt Oil, and he worked there nine years. After Hunt formed the AFL in 1959, he offered Steadman a job taking care of the financial books and basically doing whatever else that needed to be done to get the business up and running.

In 1960, impressed with his football-business acumen, Hunt offered Steadman the general manager's job. At first he was reluctant to take it because like many others he was concerned the AFL might not survive. Hunt, however, assured him that if the league went belly up he could go back to work at Hunt Oil.

With that safety net in hand, Steadman agreed to become the Texans' general manager. His personality was quite different than Hunt's as he was known for being quite brash while Hunt was more warm and welcoming.

Now throw in Stram's personality and it's easy to see why there were differences at times between the Hall of Fame coach and Steadman. But the results were largely successful as the Texans went from losing money in the AFL to eventually turning profits as the Chiefs in the NFL.

After the move, one of Steadman's first priorities was to market the Chiefs beyond Kansas City and make them a regional attraction across Kansas, Missouri, Nebraska, Oklahoma and Iowa. The Chiefs' season-ticket base increased thanks in part to allowing payment plans, an innovative idea at the time in which Steadman was one of the first football executives to implement.

After playing at Municipal Stadium from 1963 to 1971, the Chiefs moved to the Truman Sports Complex in 1972. Steadman was instrumental in the dual-purpose stadium coming to fruition. Having to share Municipal Stadium with the A's was problematic for the Chiefs. They usually spent the first few weeks of the season on the road, and they also had to deal with A's owner Charlie Finley, who was set on moving the team.

"Finley was never interested in our stadium proposals," Steadman said in *Arrowhead: Home of the Chiefs*. "Aside from making me crazy, he made us realize that we didn't want to be codependent on a team that might leave."

In June 1967, a bond issue was passed and the Chiefs and A's were granted new homes. Finley, however, moved the A's to Oakland after the 1967 baseball season. The Chiefs, meanwhile, were riding a wave of momentum having played in Super Bowl I in January and season-ticket sales went sky high.

Initially, Hunt and Steadman eyed a 70,000 seat stadium, but Hunt threw in a few more dollars, and the opening capacity of Arrowhead grew to 78,097. At the time, the Chiefs had the third-largest stadium in football, but played in the third-smallest market. Eventually the bill came due.

Downward spiral

Following the Chiefs' victory over the Vikings in Super Bowl IV, Hunt gave Steadman a 10-year contract. With it came control over most of the team's player personnel decisions, which upset Stram. The team's talent level deteriorated rapidly and so did attendance.

Following the 1974 season, Steadman fired Stram after the team went 5-9. It was the Chiefs' first losing season since 1963, their first year in Kansas City. Unfortunately, the tough times were just beginning. From 1972-1988 the Chiefs made the playoffs just once and Steadman stepped down at the end of the 1988 season to make way for a new regime.

"I have to be as responsible as anybody for that," Steadman said after he stepped down. "Like any president, I asked questions when you're not getting the results. The fact is that finally I decided the only way we were going to turn the operation around was to change from a business-run front office to a football-run front office."

Though he was no longer active in the daily operations of the Chiefs, Steadman still served as adviser to Hunt. As chairman of Hunt Midwest Enterprises, Steadman and Hunt developed many businesses in Kansas City, including Worlds of Fun and Oceans of Fun.

In 2005, Steadman was inducted into the Chiefs Hall of Fame, and he officially retired in 2007. He died on July 5, 2015.

"I had the privilege of knowing Jack my entire life, and he taught me much about both business and life," Chiefs owner Clark Hunt said after Steadman's death. "He always brought a strong, innovative perspective to the room.

"Jack was an outstanding man of character, who greatly valued his faith and family. While today we are saddened by his passing, his contributions to the Chiefs, the Kansas City community and my family will never be forgotten."

Carl Peterson spent 20 years as Chiefs president, GM and CEO. Here he is before the start of the Chiefs-Chargers game on Nov. 9, 2008, in San Diego, Calif. (Matt A. Brown/Icon Sportswire)

Carl Peterson

Perhaps enough time has gone by that we can now look at Carl Peterson's reign as Chiefs general manager in a little bit different light.

From 1989-2008 Peterson served as president, general manager and CEO of the Chiefs, and part of him wishes he was still in charge.

"I miss some of it," Peterson said during a visit to Chiefs practice in 2015. "As the president, general manager and CEO, I wore three different hats. There were parts of it that I really liked and other parts that I don't miss.

"Obviously I don't miss having to negotiate contracts with contentious agents. There are good ones out there. Aspects of it that I do miss are obviously the relationship with the coaches, the players and the fans."

At the time of his hiring, Peterson's top directive from Lamar Hunt was to fill the seats and make the game-day experience at Arrowhead the best in the NFL. A key component in that was allowing fans to tailgate before, during and after games. Doing so initially hurt the Chiefs at the concession stand, but in Peterson's mind it was a must in order to generate interest in a fan base that had watched the franchise go from Super Bowl winners to an afterthought.

In 1988, the Chiefs averaged about 50,000 fans a game. Peterson saw how empty the seats were at Arrowhead when he attended a game that season while interviewing for the soon-to-be-open GM position.

Peterson began his football career as a high school coach in California before moving to the college ranks. He was head coach at Cal State-Sonoma from 1970-71 before he returned to his alma matter, UCLA, in 1972. In 1976, Peterson followed Dick Vermeil to the Philadelphia Eagles, where Vermeil was coach and Peterson served as director of player personnel.

The 1980 Eagles team went to the Super Bowl but lost to the Raiders. When Vermeil walked away from the game after the 1982 season, Peterson became president and GM of the Philadelphia Stars of the USFL.

The Stars won the USFL championship in 1984 and 1985, but the league folded in 1986. For the next two years, Peterson fielded several calls from NFL teams, including the Jets, Chargers and Patriots. But they weren't the right fit for him. Peterson eventually found what he was looking for with the Chiefs in December 88—complete control over the organization.

Under Peterson the Chiefs began looking at the business side through a new lens, one that emphasized winning games and not only the dollars. His first big move was hiring Marty Schottenheimer, who had just been fired by the Cleveland Browns after leading them to the AFC championship game twice.

Peterson and Schottenheimer each valued strong defensive teams, and together they rebuilt the Chiefs quickly—fueled by drafting Derrick Thomas with the fourth overall pick in the 1989 NFL Draft. Chiefs fans didn't know it at the time, but after enduring years of misery, in a matter of months they had three organizational pillars in place who would change the franchise forever.

In Peterson's second year, the Chiefs' average attendance climbed to 60,000 a game. By his third season, the Chiefs were averaging 75,000 fans every Sunday, and Peterson had been given the nickname "King Carl."

The Chiefs made the playoffs three straight years (1990-92) but were in need of some offensive upgrades if they were going to "reach the Super Bowl within five years," as was Peterson's original plan. So in 1993, Peterson traded for Joe Montana and brought in free agent running back Marcus Allen, two moves that took the team's popularity to another level.

The Chiefs reached the AFC championship game that season, the first time since 1969. But Peterson's five-year plan never got that close again. Even though the Chiefs were the No. 1 seed in the playoffs twice in the 1990s—first in 1995 and again in 1997—they lost their opening game each time.

The Chiefs went a disappointing 7-9 in 1998, marking the team's first losing record in the Peterson-Schottenheimer era. Schottenheimer resigned shortly after the season and just like that a beautiful 10-year marriage was over.

Peterson picked defensive coordinator Gunther Cunningham as Schottenheimer's replacement. That lasted two years as Cunningham learned he was being fired—and replaced by Vermeil—while surfing the internet early one morning while working in his office at Arrowhead.

At Vermeil's introductory news conference, Peterson described him as "the premier coach in the National Football League." At the time, Vermeil was just one year removed from winning the Super Bowl as coach of the Rams.

But the Chiefs made the playoffs just once in Vermeil's five years at the helm despite having an offense that set records. When Vermeil retired Peterson traded for New York Jets coach Herm Edwards. He was tasked to make one last run at a Super Bowl then lead the upcoming youth movement.

When neither of those worked out, Clark Hunt decided a change was needed, and Peterson stepped down following a dismal 2-14 season in 2008, ending one of the longer tenures in recent sports history.

Peterson's legacy with the team, however, is a little complicated. The Chiefs went 176-141-1, won four AFC West titles and he drafted three Hall of Famers in a span of 20 years. But the ending is often what people remember most. And to that end, he's remembered as this polarizing figure who was difficult to deal with at times, howled at the local media a little too often, and left the team somewhat on bad terms.

Still, he is one of the most influential people in team history, and the man most responsible for creating a brand of football that resonated with the fans and still does today. And that's something worth remembering.

"This is—and I said it when I was running the Chiefs for 20 years—the best, the greatest fan base in all of the NFL as far as I'm concerned," Peterson said. "They're great Chiefs fans, and I certainly will always be a Chiefs fan."

John Dorsey

It's not often you make the playoffs three times in your first four seasons on job and get fired. But that's what happened to John Dorsey.

Dorsey was given his walking papers from owner Clark Hunt on June 22, 2017, while the Chiefs were already well into the fifth year of the Andy Reid-John Dorsey era. The timing of the dismissal was not ideal, and ironically Dorsey's firing came just hours after the Chiefs announced a contract extension with Reid.

"I want to thank Clark, the Hunt family and the Chiefs fans for the opportunity to be a part of Chiefs Kingdom over the last four seasons," Dorsey said in a statement after he was let go. "I believe this team is well positioned for the future and I wish Coach Reid, the players and the entire organization all the best."

Dorsey and Reid were viewed as a power couple after they arrived in January 2013. The Chiefs were coming off a horrendous 2-14 season but their fortunes quickly turned for the better.

Dorsey arrived in Kansas City nine days after Hunt tabbed Reid as coach, and he came with quite a pedigree. Dorsey began his NFL career as a linebacker with the Packers in 1984 before he moved to the front office in 1991.

In 1992, Reid joined the Packers as an assistant coach, and he and Dorsey worked together for the next seven years. In 1999, Dorsey began a two-year stint as director of player personnel with Seattle while Reid became head coach of the Eagles.

Dorsey then returned to Green Bay and worked his way up the ladder. At the time of his hiring by the Chiefs, he was viewed somewhat as a savior, considering what the Chiefs had just gone through under Scott Pioli.

Pioli arrived via the Super Bowl coattails of Bill Belichick and Tom Brady in 2009 and was considered the NFL's rising star among those in front office circles. But a deep disconnect with newly-hired head coach Todd Haley quickly formed and a toxic work environment soon engulfed Arrowhead Stadium, largely because of Pioli's paranoia.

Haley believed Pioli had his cellphone and office bugged, and other employees had the same concerns. Once Pioli noticed a candy wrapper in a stairwell and waited around to see how long it took for someone to pick it up.

After guiding the Chiefs to the playoffs and a division title in 2010, Haley was fired with three games to go in the 2011 season. He was replaced by defensive coordinator Romeo Crennel and somehow the Chiefs won two of their last three games. Pioli then removed Crennel's interim label and he coached the team through 2012.

Though the issues the Chiefs had with Dorsey weren't quite to the extent of Pioli's, they were severe enough that Hunt—after saying Dorsey and Reid likely would both get contract extensions—backtracked a few months later after he conducted an internal review of the football operations department.

Unlike Pioli before him, Dorsey's drafts have already proven to be pretty solid. However, the team was in a salary-cap nightmare and there were issues with Dorsey's communication—or lack thereof with people in the organization—and his management style, especially handling the release of veterans Jamaal Charles and Jeremy Maclin.

Charles, the franchise's all-time leading rusher, was never given the opportunity to restructure his deal. And Maclin, who grew up a few hours outside Kansas City, starred at Missouri and played his first four seasons for Reid with Eagles, found out he was being released in a voicemail from Dorsey one day after practice.

Neither move went over well with fans, and by that time Hunt already had concerns about giving Dorsey an extension. When Hunt decided he would not retain Dorsey after the final year of his contract, he chose to fire him rather than have him work as a lame-duck GM.

"Over the course of the spring there were enough issues that popped up that caused me to want to do a full evaluation of the football department before I extended either Andy or John," Hunt said a month after Dorsey was fired. "In the course of that evaluation I just became concerned about our ability to continue the success that we've had the last four years, or better yet, to build on that success and have a championship team."

Cleveland hired Dorsey as GM that December. The Browns finished 0-16 that year, but in his first full season in 2018 the Browns went 7-8-1. Dorsey also signed running back Kareem Hunt after he was released by the Chiefs.

Brett Veach

The job of a new general manager oftentimes is to shake things up. Brett Veach has done that, but how fast he's done it is what really stands out.

Veach was named Chiefs general manager on July 10, 2017, just a few weeks after Clark Hunt relieved John Dorsey of his duties. Since then Veach has infused the roster with a much-needed dose of speed and toughness, proving already that he's one of, if not the most aggressive GMs in team history.

"My strength would be in the college draft and player acquisition," Veach said. "When I knew I wanted to be a GM, you knew the salary cap is an important part of this. It's a very important aspect. But the cap is very specialized, so I know relative value. My job is to articulate the plan, the vision for the next two or three years."

Chiefs general manager Brett Veach's vision for success is founded upon building the team through the draft. Here he is speaking to the media at the NFL Scouting Combine on Feb. 28, 2019, in Indianapolis. (Robin Alam/Icon Sportswire)

A big part of that vision focuses on youth, most notably quarterback Patrick Mahomes. When the Chiefs drafted Mahomes, Veach was co-director of player personnel and he had already been raving about the Texas Tech quarterback to coach Andy Reid for some time.

"I thought he was the best quarterback draft in the draft, absolutely," Veach said.

Mahomes has proven Veach right. And as the youngest GM in the NFL, Veach has hit on several other big decisions, including turning over an aging roster that won two straight division titles but probably reached its peak following another home playoff loss to the Titans in January 2018.

A few weeks later, Veach began a series of deals that led to several mainstays departing the organization. Alex Smith was traded to the Redskins, Marcus Peters was traded to the Rams, and Derrick Johnson and Tamba Hali were not brought back.

The Chiefs acquired Kendall Fuller in the Smith trade and signed linebacker Anthony Hitchens and wide receiver Sammy Watkins, both of whom Veach tried to trade for shortly after he was named GM.

"It goes back to core philosophies," Veach said. "You have core philosophies in every transactional period. So you have core philosophies in the draft, you have core philosophies in the free agency period and one of those is guys that are young that can grow and develop with your culture and with your vision for this team.

"Listen, it's a tough, violent league, and the more wear and tear you have the harder it is to produce and play. And the younger you are the more juice you have. And those young guys, would the level of interest have been the same if they were 30 years old? No."

Veach grew up in Mount Carmel, Pa., and earned a scholarship from Delaware, where he was a running back, receiver and kick returner. Working as a grad assistant, Veach landed a summer internship with Reid and the Eagles in 2004. Veach made such an impression on Reid that in 2006 he was hired as Reid's assistant. The two have worked together ever since.

"He's relentless," Reid said of Veach. "That energy isn't coming out of a can or something. That's real, and he's that way 24-7. He goes and goes."

With two division titles, a playoff win and a young and improving team, the future is definitely bright for the Chiefs.

"We look forward to the future," Veach said. "Coach (Reid) and I both feel that we've plotted a course to turn a new chapter for this organization and we're excited."

CHAPTER 4
THE COACHES

Hank Stram

The Chiefs have been blessed with several outstanding head coaches over the years, but Hank Stram was truly one of a kind.

Always well-dressed and quite jovial in manner, Stram coached the Texans/Chiefs from 1960-74, leading the franchise to AFL championships in 1962, 1966 and 1969, and the Super Bowl title in January 1970. The Chiefs' all-time winningest coach, Stram went 124-76-10 in 15 seasons working for Lamar Hunt. The two shared a great bond despite having completely different upbringings and personalities.

Hunt grew up surrounded by wealth while Stram grew up in poverty. Stram also was a round and talkative fellow while Hunt was skinny and a man of few words. But the two had one thing in common—football.

It's hard to imagine the Chiefs history without Stram, but he wasn't Hunt's first choice to run his new team. Stram was actually third on Hunt's list, behind legendary Oklahoma coach Bud Wilkinson and a rising New York Giants assistant named Tom Landry.

Both Wilkinson and Landry had reservations about joining a new league so when they told Hunt no, he turned his attention to Stram, who had a fine reputation in the college ranks and was known as one of the game's most forward thinkers.

Stram carried that reputation with him throughout his pro career.

He was a master tactician on offense, defense and special teams, pioneering the rolling pocket, the I-formation, two-tight end sets, and the 3-4, triple-stack and zone defenses, just to name a few.

Short in stature but large on life, Stram became friends with Muhammad Ali and even tried to convince Wilt Chamberlain to play football for him in Kansas City. But it was on the biggest stage when Stram shined brightest as he gave the NFL and generations of Chiefs lasting memories in a Hall of Fame career.

The Mentor

Stram was born Henry Louis Wilczek on Jan. 3, 1923, in Chicago. His father, also named Henry, worked as a clothing salesman and tailor and wrestled under the surname of Stram, which later became the family's legal name.

Stram was just 9 when his father died, leaving his mother, Nellie, to raise him and his two sisters. Stram attended Lew Wallace High School in Gary, Ind. He ran track and played basketball and baseball, but football was his calling. He became an All-State halfback and got a scholarship from Purdue University.

Stram played running back for the Boilermakers in 1942, and like many in those days he had to leave school to serve in World War II. He served in the Army Air Forces and returned to college in 1946 and graduated in 1948. Stram was an assistant on the football team until 1955, and he also coached the baseball team from 1951-55.

At Purdue, Stram coached future Texans/Chiefs quarterback Len Dawson before becoming an assistant at SMU, Notre Dame and Miami. One day in the spring of 1959, he received a call from Hunt, who wanted to gauge his interest in possibly coaching his team in the new football league he was starting.

Stram didn't know much about Hunt at that point, but Miami coach Andy Gustafson had heard of him. When he told Stram that Hunt was one of the richest people in the world, Stram's eyes lit up.

Kansas City Chiefs coach Hank Stram watches his team during a game against the Oakland Raiders on Nov. 23, 1969, at Municipal Stadium in Kansas City, Mo. "The Mentor" was always well-dressed and led the Chiefs to a win against the Vikings in Super Bowl IV. (Kenneth Spencer Research Library, University of Kansas Libraries)

During spring practice, Hunt flew to Miami to meet with Stram. Stram kept looking up into the stands to find Hunt, whom he believed would be well-dressed for such an occasion. The two had actually met before in 1956 when Stram was an assistant at SMU, but he couldn't remember what Hunt looked like.

As Stram was walking off the field after practice, Hunt called down to him from the stands. Stram, as he recalled in his autobiography *They're Playing My Game*, looked up and saw "a man wearing horn-rimmed glasses and a rumpled raincoat."

Hunt introduced himself, and the two began chatting.

"He was very polite and pleasant," Stram continued in his book. "I liked him right away. He suggested that we go to dinner, and we talked some more. When the check came, Hunt reached into his pocket and sighed. He exclaimed that he was embarrassed at not having any money on him.

"He asked me to pay the bill and (said) that he would reimburse me later. I couldn't believe it. Andy had been telling me how rich the guy was and yet he couldn't pay for dinner. I began to wonder."

Stram's doubts continued as months passed and he hadn't heard another word from Hunt. Later that November, Stram was giving a speech at his high school when a waiter told him he had an important phone call from Texas.

Hunt wanted Stram to meet him in Dallas the next day, but Stram had a speaking engagement scheduled in Chicago. So Hunt found a way to make the logistics work and promised Stram that he would drive him back to the airport in time so he could make his flight to Chicago.

At the meeting in Dallas, they didn't talk about money or even a contract. But the opportunity to mold a new franchise appealed to Stram. After the meeting, Hunt had a few important business calls that he needed to make so he asked Stram if he would bring his car around to save time.

Stram walked to the parking lot a few blocks away and expected to see the attendant pull up in a Rolls Royce. Instead, Stram wound up driving back a rusted-out Oldsmobile 88 that had a big hole in the front seat.

A few days later, Hunt called Stram and offered him a job as his football coach. Hunt offered him a three-year contract that paid $15,000 a year. Stram, however, said he wouldn't take it unless he made $20,000 a year.

Stram was only making about $7,000 at Miami, but he had already been offered the head coaching job at Wichita State, which Hunt didn't know about. Later that day, Hunt called Stram back and upped his offer to $20,000, and Stram couldn't say no.

In the late 1950s and early '60s, most offenses utilized a power running game. But Stram believed if the AFL was going to compete with the NFL for fan interest, it would need a new style of play. And who better to implement it than the 36-year-old Stram?

With his game plan wrapped in his right hand, Stram's motion offenses confused defenses, and his teams consistently ranked at or near the top of the league in yards gained. In his first season in Dallas, Stram coached the Texans to an 8-6 record, good for second place behind the Los Angeles Chargers. Running back Abner Haynes rushed for 875 yards and nine touchdowns and caught 55 passes for 576 yards and three scores as he became the league's first Rookie of the Year and league MVP.

In 1962 with Dawson at quarterback, the Texans went 11-3 and defeated the Houston Oilers in the AFL championship game. Around that time Dawson was thinking about buying a house in Dallas, but Stram told him it would be wise to wait.

When the franchise moved to Kansas City, it was common for the home team's bench to be on the same side of the field as the press box. The TV cameras therefore showed mostly the backs of the players on the sideline and not their faces, and that's if they got any camera time at all. Stram, however, strategically put his team on the other side of the field so he and the Chiefs could get more TV time.

Courting Wilt

In 1964, Stram believed he could turn NBA superstar Wilt Chamberlain into a star wide receiver for the Chiefs. Chamberlain was receptive to the idea and even had a workout with Stram in upstate New York.

Chamberlain, who played for the San Francisco Warriors at the time, stood 7-foot-1 and weighed 290 pounds. By the end of the practice, Stram was mesmerized with the former University of Kansas basketball and track star.

"I'm certain from what I saw he would be the greatest flanker back in football," Stram told the Associated Press. "Wilt and I had quite a talk. He's interested, genuinely interested.

"He took off his shoes and shirt and was just wearing his slacks, silk pants. I started throwing him some passes to his left, to his right, over the goalposts. He caught everything I threw. And then I clocked him in the 40-yard dash. He ran a 4.6 barefooted."

Haynes, who was one of the fastest players in the AFL, could run it in 4.7 seconds, according to the article. So imagine, for a moment, Dawson throwing passes to Chamberlain.

"With his size, his speed, his range, there isn't a defensive back in the world who could even come close to containing him," Stram continued. "You could put him out on a corner, and he and our quarterback could just play catch."

Stram wanted to sign Chamberlain, who was making $50,000 a year playing in the NBA, but the Warriors wouldn't allow it, and so the "Big Dipper" never played in the NFL. Stram, however, stayed on the lookout for a similar-sized player, and in 1969 he drafted 6-foot-10 Morris Stroud, a basketball player from Clark Atlanta University, an all-black school in Atlanta.

Stroud had very little experience playing football, but Stram told him that he was going to play tight end and on special teams. Stroud played six seasons with the Chiefs, catching 54 passes for 977 yards and seven touchdowns. But what Stram had him to do on special teams created a stir in the NFL.

On field goals, Stram strategically placed Stroud beneath the goalpost. His job was to jump up and swat the ball down, taking three points off the scoreboard for the opponent. There's no record of Stroud actually doing this successfully in a game, but he came close a time or two. So the NFL instituted the "Stroud Rule," which states "goaltending by any player leaping up to deflect a kick as it passes above the crossbar is prohibited. The referee could award three points for a palpably unfair act."

Wired for sound

Dawson was the MVP of Super Bowl IV, but Stram was the star. Prior to the game, NFL Films had a grand idea—get Stram to become the first coach in history to wear a microphone during the Super Bowl. NFL Films thought Stram would be perfect with his sideline strut and humorous one-liners so they offered him $500.

Stram rejected the initial offer, saying "That wouldn't pay my dry-cleaning bill!" After some further negotiations, Stram agreed to do it for $1,000. What happened next was priceless. Stram, dressed in a black blazer and tie with a red vest and matching silk handkerchief, had the time of his life laughing, smiling, and saying gems like "Just keep matriculating the ball down the field, boys," and "That's like stealing!" as his offense went up and down the field against the Vikings.

Stram's most memorable moment occurred when he called what would become the most famous play in team history. Up 9-0 in the second quarter, the Chiefs had the ball at the Minnesota 5-yard line. Stram had a hunch that a play his team hadn't practiced in weeks might work so he called for "65 Toss Power Trap."

The play's design went like this: "Sixty" was the offensive formation, "five" was the hole running back Mike Garrett was supposed to run through, "Power" meant that tight end Fred Arbanas would block down on the middle linebacker and "Trap" meant that right guard Mo Moorman would pull to the left and take out the defensive end.

So Stram grabbed wide receiver Gloster Richardson off the bench and sent him into the huddle with instruction for Dawson.

"Gloster, tell him '65 Toss Power Trap,'" Stram said.

In the huddle, Dawson couldn't believe it. So he asked Richardson if he was sure that's what Stram wanted to run. Richardson said yes, and Stram watched intently from the sideline.

"It might pop wide open," Stram said just before E.J. Holub snapped the ball to Dawson.

The play worked to perfection. Garrett ran into the end zone nearly untouched, giving the Chiefs a 16-0 lead and essentially icing the game right there. On the sideline, a joyous Stram laughed and celebrated with his team.

"I tell you that baby was there!" he shouted. "Yes, sir, boys! Whoo!"

At the game's conclusion, Stram's players hoisted him up and carried him off the field. The Chiefs had won convincingly 23-7, and Stram was at the top of the mountain, right where he belonged. Sadly, the Chiefs never reached the pinnacle again under Stram and he was fired following the 1974 season. Parting ways with the only head coach the franchise had ever known was extremely difficult for Hunt, who in the early days of the Chiefs stayed at Stram's house to save on hotels and later asked him to be the best man at his wedding to Norma.

Hunt would later regret firing Stram, who coached again with the Saints but was let go after two consecutive losing seasons. After retiring from coaching, he enjoyed a long broadcasting career with CBS. For 18 years, Stram called Monday Night Football games with Jack Buck on the radio. He also worked with Vin Scully and Jim Nantz on TV.

As a broadcaster, Stram saw the game through a coach's eye and often predicted what was about to unfold before the play began. He even somewhat foreshadowed "The Catch" from Joe Montana to Dwight Clark in the 1981 NFC championship game, saying "We'll see a pick of some kind on the right side possibly" just before Montana took the snap and rolled right.

Clark was indeed supposed to set a pick for 49ers wide receiver Freddie Solomon, who was Montana's first read. But Solomon fell down on the play, and Montana had to hold the ball a little longer until finally he floated a pass to Clark in the back of the end zone.

Stram was inducted into the Chiefs Hall of Fame in 1987 but it took until 2003 for him to be enshrined in the Pro Football Hall of Fame. At that time, his health was fading and he was in a wheelchair. He died two years later, but in many ways he's still with us as many of his principles, philosophies and formations are still evident in today's NFL. And that would surely make Hank smile.

Marty Schottenheimer

Lamar Hunt once said "the golden era" of Chiefs football was when Marty Schottenheimer walked the sidelines as head coach. From 1989-98, the Schottenheimer-led Chiefs went 101-58-1 in the regular season and won three AFC West titles.

With tough, hard-nosed and hard-hitting football teams that ran the ball and played defense, Schottenheimer revitalized a franchise and won over a fan base that he connected with so well because of his gritty roots, strong work ethic and passionate, pregame and postgame speeches.

Whether it was instructing his team to "take the bull by the horns and wrestle it to the ground," or take it "one play at a time," Schottenheimer's message always came straight from the heart. His players adored him from the moment they met. And now 30 years later their love for him is never ending, and their thoughts are with him constantly as he battles Alzheimer's with the strength that only a Schottenheimer can.

Schottenheimer enjoyed unbelievable success as an NFL head coach for 21 seasons, first with the Browns and Chiefs and later the Redskins and Chargers. With it came heartbreaking playoff defeats that sometimes unfairly overshadowed his greatness as a teacher, winner and leader of men.

Schottenheimer is widely considered one of the greatest coaches in NFL history and is in the top 10 in career wins. Yet he is not in the Pro Football Hall of Fame, an unfortunate penalty for not winning the big one. He is, however, a beloved figure to Chiefs fans and his place in team history is secure.

Chiefs coach Marty Schottenheimer enlightens his team during a game against the Chargers on Nov. 22, 1998, in San Diego. Schottenheimer won 101 games in the regular season in his 10 years as coach of the Chiefs but went just 3-7 in the playoffs. (John Cordes/Icon Sportswire)

The Dawg Pound

Born on Sept. 23, 1943, in Canonsburg, Pa., Martin Edward Schottenheimer played defensive tackle for Fort Cherry High School in McDonald, Pa., and earned a scholarship from the University of Pittsburgh.

Schottenheimer was moved to linebacker and started all four years at Pitt. In 1965, he was selected in the fourth round of the NFL Draft by the Baltimore Colts and the seventh round by the Buffalo Bills of the AFL. Schottenheimer chose to sign with the Bills and played four seasons there. As a rookie, he helped the Bills win the AFL title and was selected to the AFL All-Star team.

One time against the New York Jets, Schottenheimer missed a tackle on longtime friend Joe Namath. Upset by the play, Schottenheimer let it affect him the rest of the drive, and the Jets wound up scoring a touchdown. Afterward, Schottenheimer swore he wouldn't let it happen again, and his mantra "one play at a time" was born.

Schottenheimer was traded to the Boston Patriots in 1969 and he spent two seasons there. He was traded to the Steelers in 1971 and traded again to the Colts before the start of the regular season but decided to retire from football and became a real estate agent.

When that career didn't pan out, he got back into football, first as a player/coach for the Portland Thunder of the World Football League in 1974. The league eventually went bankrupt, and Schottenheimer was out of work after one season. His wife, Pat, supported the family for a while before he got a job as linebackers coach with the New York Giants. Two years later, he became the team's defensive coordinator and later became an assistant with the Lions.

In 1980, Schottenheimer was named defensive coordinator of the Browns. He directed the defense for four and a half years until he became head coach halfway through the 1984 season. The Browns were 1-7 when Schottenheimer took over but went 4-4 in the second half.

With Schottenheimer in charge, the Browns won the division the next three years and made the AFC championship game in 1986 and 1987, losing both times to John Elway and the Broncos as "The Drive" and "The Fumble" became part of pop culture.

Schottenheimer won 44 games in four and a half seasons as Cleveland's coach, but owner Art Modell wanted him to fire some of his assistants following the 1988 season in which the Browns went 10-6 and lost in the first round of the playoffs. When Schottenheimer refused, he and Modell mutually agreed to part ways. A few weeks later, Carl Peterson brought Schottenheimer to Kansas City, and the Chiefs were soon up and running.

A hit from the start

When Schottenheimer arrived in Kansas City in January 1989, he first met with each player individually. Nick Lowery had already made the Pro Bowl twice and was the best kicker in the NFL. Lowery played collegiately at Dartmouth of the Ivy League and was known for being one of the most intelligent players in the game, something Schottenheimer was well aware of.

"He said, 'Nick, you're smart. The problem is you're too smart. You think too much,' Lowery recalled. "And he said with kickers, 'I'm going to coach them like you either make it or you don't. If you make it, you'll be with me. If you don't, you won't.' He was very straightforward, and I loved that it was all about hard work, loyalty to the team and then production."

Lowery had his best seasons after Schottenheimer became coach, those coming after he turned 34.

"Marty just made us feel like a tough, professional united team," Lowery said. "He helped us always stay on the same page, which is what a great leader does."

When Schottenheimer addressed the team for the first time, Lowery watched intently from the front row.

"I'll never forget that first day he was speaking to us," Lowery said. "Carl Peterson got up and said, 'Vince Lombardi said winning was a habit, but so also is losing.' And Marty got up, and his hands were shaking. And I was like, 'Man, this guy cares so much.' He literally shook with emotion of what he was trying to say.

"And that's why you are loyal as a player for a coach like Marty because you knew he truly cared. And to that end, he was not like Dick Vermeil, who would give you a big hug, and maybe even kiss you. Now Dick Vermeil was an awesome coach, but they were very different that way. Marty, he withheld that, but you also knew under that he did care. And you could see it in real time."

One of those moments came when the Chiefs were playing San Diego, and as Eric Bieniemy broke free on a kick return, Lowery's eyes widened as he moved in to make the tackle.

"I had to hit this 5-foot-8, 220-pound bowling ball and try to get him out of the way so we have a chance to prevent a touchdown," Lowery said. "And so I had my single-bar helmet, and my shoulder pads, and I ran and hit him.

"He hit me so hard—it was right by the sidelines—and he launched me 5 yards in the air, and I landed on my left side. I could feel all the air coming out of my lungs, and I was like, 'Uggh!' I found out later I had cracked ribs. And Marty ran right over, and it was like, 'He does care. I like that.' Anyway, that means a lot to you."

That season, the Chiefs weren't blessed with a potent offense. Lowery led the league in field goal percentage at 91.7 percent, making 22 of 24 attempts. But even back then, 22 field goals weren't considered a lot, and Lowery wasn't sure he'd make the Pro Bowl.

On the day the AFC squad was announced—a time before the internet boom—Lowery and punter/holder Bryan Barker were practicing field goals a half hour before practice. Lowery hadn't heard anything about being selected so he figured he didn't make it.

"It was a gray, cold day at the Chiefs practice field facility, and Bryan goes, 'Uh oh! There's Marty, he's coming out early,'" Lowery said. "Our first thing was, 'What did we do wrong?' And we're on the far field, and he's walking across, and he comes over with this beautiful poker face, which was broken by a smile.

"He goes, 'Hey, Nick, congratulations. You made the Pro Bowl.' I will never forget that. I will never forget what a dear, caring guy. He's someone that I will love my whole life."

Martyball

To most Chiefs fans, "Martyball" invokes memories of a power running game. To Schottenheimer, Martyball simply meant winning any way possible.

With Bernie Kosar quarterbacking the Browns, Schottenheimer's offenses were strong through the air. In 1986, Kosar's second season in the NFL, he threw for 3,854 yards and 17 touchdowns. In 1987, the Browns were fifth in passing yards and 21st running the ball. In Schottenheimer's final season in Cleveland in 1988, the Browns were ninth in passing and 24th rushing.

That all changed when he became coach of the Chiefs. Schottenheimer always loved big backs. In Cleveland, he had Kevin Mack. In Kansas City, he had Christian Okoye, a bruising 260-pounder who could run a 4.45.

Though Okoye was still pretty new to football—he was a 26-year-old rookie in 1987—he probably was underused his first two seasons with the Chiefs. Schottenheimer, however, fed him the ball constantly. In 1989, Okoye led the NFL with 370 carries. His previous career-high was 157 as a rookie. Okoye led the league in rushing with 1,480 yards in 1989, often heeding Schottenheimer's call to "get low" and "make a hole" when there wasn't one.

The Chiefs went 8-7-1 that season behind Okoye and Rookie of the Year linebacker Derrick Thomas, who had 10 sacks.

"He's an exception rather than the rule because he has all the natural athletic skills and instincts and desire to be successful," Schottenheimer said of Thomas in 1989.

Schottenheimer had gotten to know a few Chiefs players from having coached them in the Pro Bowl when he was in Cleveland. One of them was six-time Pro Bowl safety Deron Cherry.

"I played in two Pro Bowl games for Marty in Hawaii and so I knew him pretty well," Cherry said. "I knew how stubborn he was and how strong minded he was. I remember when he was in Cleveland they always had problems playing the Broncos, that was his big thing.

"I remember I'm sitting in the film room one night and I'm studying film after practice. I'm the only one there and Dave Kendall, our trainer, comes in and says I have a phone call. And I didn't know who was calling me at the stadium after practice so I go in there and answer the phone and it's Tom Pratt."

Pratt was the Chiefs defensive line coach in Super Bowl IV and was Schottenheimer's defensive line coach at the time.

"He goes, 'I got Coach Schottenheimer here, and he wants to talk to you,'" Cherry recalled. "And so I go, 'Hi, Marty.' And he proceeds to ask me a bunch of questions on how he's been watching film of us playing the Denver Broncos and John Elway, and he was wanting to get some tips on what we did to Elway that made us so successful as a secondary, and I proceeded to tell him. And he goes, 'Thank you, I appreciate it.'

"I don't think it would have happened if I didn't have that kind of relationship with him, or if he didn't have that kind of respect for me. When you play two games for a guy over there, you really get to know him because it's more of a relaxed atmosphere. But the fact that he had that much respect to call me and say what do I need to do against Elway that'll create problems for him and why do you guys have so much success. Nowadays coaches don't do that, but back in the day they did."

Like Cherry, fellow Chiefs Hall of Fame safety Lloyd Burruss only played three years for Schottenheimer. Burruss had been a starter since his rookie season in 1981, but age and injuries pushed him into a backup role when Schottenheimer became coach.

"Marty was by far the best coach I ever had," Burruss said. "When Marty came to Kansas City, we started winning football and football became great fun. That's the way he was. Marty was very emotional, he was passionate and emotional with it. I can remember them making me come back out to stand up and say I was going to retire, which I didn't want to do.

"I wanted to just go off into the sunset, and him and Carl Peterson, they got me back out there. They made me come back out, and I was up there standing in front of the team announcing my retirement, that I'm going to give it up. And I turn around and look over at Marty and he has tears in his eyes. That kind of thing, it hits you. It shows he cares. It's something that you put inside your soul and your spirit and you just hold it for the rest of your life. You live with things like that, it meant something to him. He was very passionate. You could tell he was no phony."

Case for Canton

After a disastrous 1998 season in which the Chiefs had Super Bowl hopes but finished 7-9, Schottenheimer resigned as coach. It was the first losing season of his head coaching career, and the season itself, combined with past playoff defeats, became too much to bear.

Hunt tried to talk him out of it and stay on as coach, but Schottenheimer felt he needed to step away. It was a decision he would later come to regret.

After spending two years as an analyst on ESPN, Schottenheimer became coach of the Redskins in 2001. The Redskins lost their first five games but still finished 8-8. Schottenheimer, though, was fired after just one season. He coached the Chargers from 2002-06 and won 47 games but went 0-2 in the playoffs and was fired.

In 21 seasons as a head coach, Schottenheimer won 200 games in the regular season and had a losing record just twice. But he went just 5-13 in the postseason and didn't win another playoff game after Joe Montana and the Chiefs beat the Oilers.

Schottenheimer is eighth on the all-time wins list including postseason, having been passed by Chiefs coach Andy Reid last season. Five of the top six are in the Hall of Fame. The other—Bill Belichick—will be when he retires. Schottenheimer, though, has never been a finalist.

His 93 wins are the most of any coach in the 1990s, and here's a breakdown of the quarterbacks who started for him during his 10 seasons in Kansas City.

Player	Win-Loss-Tie	Year(s)
Steve DeBerg	27-14	1989-91
Ron Jaworski	1-2	1989
Steve Pelluer	1-1-1	1989
Mark Vlasic	0-1	1991
Dave Krieg	13-8	1992-93
Joe Montana	17-8	1993-94
Steve Bono	21-10	1994-96
Rich Gannon	11-8	1995-98
Elvis Grbac	10-6	1997-98

DeBerg was his longest-tenured starter in Kansas City at just three years, and he also had the most wins (27). But nine different quarterbacks started while Schottenheimer was coach of the Chiefs, and the instability and often mediocre play at the most important position on the field kept Schottenheimer from reaching the Super Bowl with the Chiefs.

"That's the problem with Marty," said Rick Gosselin, who has covered the NFL for more than 40 years and serves on the Hall of Fame selection committee and the contributor and senior sub-committees. "There are 20 coaches in the Hall of Fame, 17 won championships, and the three that didn't—Marv Levy went to four Super Bowls, Bud Grant went to four Super Bowls and George Allen went to one.

"Marty never got there. Marty's in the same boat with Chuck Knox and Dan Reeves—great coaches who never won a championship. And winning a championship, coaches and quarterbacks are judged on their championships and therein lies the problem."

Schottenheimer was inducted into the Chiefs Hall of Fame in 2010 and said at the time that was "the highlight" of his coaching career.

'Tough disease'

In 1986, "Top Gun" was a summer blockbuster. Schotteneheimer's daughter, Kristen, saw the movie and immediately wanted to learn how to fly. For her high school graduation, Schottenheimer agreed to let her take flying lessons—if he could take them with her.

Schottenheimer immediately fell in love with flying. On Saturdays before home games, he often flew his plane right over Arrowhead Stadium.

"There's really nothing quite as exhilarating as flying," Schottenheimer said in his autobiography *Martyball!* "You're up there above everything else. It is so peaceful, so serene. I mean, to be able to fly, that was a trip."

Several years ago, Burruss was on a flight from Kansas City headed home to Virginia. Schottenheimer and his wife, who live in Charlotte, N.C., were on the same flight. Burruss noticed that his former coach needed some assistance, and he could tell "something wasn't right." But he didn't know what at the time.

In 2016, it was revealed that Schottenheimer has been battling Alzheimer's since 2011. The incurable disease robs people of precious memories and thinking capability. Schottenheimer has taken part in clinical trials to help with treatment, and according to his family he's "doing OK," all things considered.

Marty flew with his family to Seattle for the Chiefs-Seahawks game in Week 16 last year to see his son, Brian, who followed in his father's footsteps and became a coach. Brian is now in his second season as offensive coordinator for the Seahawks.

On the trip, Schottenheimer, with Pat at his side, recorded a video commemorating Reid on passing him on the all-time wins list, a heartfelt honor from one Chief to another.

"He was on that day so he was able to congratulate Andy, and the place went crazy, I guess," Brian said at the time. "I obviously wasn't there, but Kansas City holds a dear place in our family's heart.

"He's doing OK. This will be the first road game that he'll be able to attend. He's coming in for Christmas, so he's doing OK. Tough disease, but we're excited to see him."

Gunther Cunningham

Fire and heart. Family and football. Gunther Cunningham's life personified all of those. With his unmistakable colored lenses and gravelly voice, Cunningham was one of the most respected coaches in the NFL and a treasure so rare that there will never be another like him.

Cunningham didn't do coach speak. He said what he honestly believed and he was rarely—if ever—PC. Cunningham coached in the NFL for over 30 years and 11 of those were with the Chiefs, nine as a defensive coordinator and two as a head coach. His death on May 11, 2019, after a short bout with cancer came as a surprise to many. Cunningham had lived a full life, but at age 72 he was far too young to be taken so soon.

Cunningham was born on June 9, 1946, in Munich, Germany, just a few miles from Dachau concentration camp. Dachau was the first Nazi concentration camp to open and more than 32,000 people were killed there from 1933 to April 1945 when it was liberated by U.S. forces.

Cunningham never knew his biological father. He was raised by his mother, Katharina, and stepfather, Garner, who was a sergeant in the U.S. Air Force. They met while he was stationed in Germany.

Cunningham came to the U.S. when he was 10 and couldn't speak a word of English. Eventually the family settled in Lompoc, Calif., and he fell in love with football and became a linebacker and kicker at Oregon. He then became an assistant coach at Oregon, Arkansas, Stanford and California before spending a season in the CFL.

Cunningham joined the NFL ranks in 1982 and became well known for his blitzing and physical defenses, which made him a perfect fit for Marty Schottenheimer's staff in Kansas City. He joined the Chiefs prior to the 1995 season and served as defensive coordinator until 1998. An integral part of some of Schottenheimer's best teams, Cunningham replaced Schottenheimer as head coach when Schottenheimer resigned after the 1998 season.

At his introductory press conference, Cunningham vowed he would get the Chiefs back on the right path.

"In this last year the Chiefs lost their way a little bit," Cunningham said then. "I think it's like walking through a forest, and we took the wrong path. But I will tell you this there is no doubt in my mind where the right path is, and we're going to find it, and we're going to go down that path and rekindle what needs to be rekindled in this football program."

On the first day of training camp, he showed the team "Saving Private Ryan" and talked about sacrifice.

"I saw that movie this summer, and what a great thing our country has done to keep us all free and give us the opportunity to work like we all are doing right now, and it really made an impact on me," Cunningham told reporters then. "I said a lot of things for three hours, and the last thing I did was put that movie on. Didn't show the whole thing, we just showed Omaha Beach."

During press conferences Cunningham was rather mild-mannered, but during practice and games his intensity rose to another level. And so did his colorful language. Once during training camp in his first season as Chiefs head coach, TV cameras captured him shouting to his team, "There ain't no fucking way I'm going to back off!"

Cunningham also was known to flip off the referees and shout at unruly fans both when he was defensive coordinator and head coach. But everything he did was out of love. And oh, how he loved the Chiefs.

"I made this statement when I got to Kansas City that I found utopia," Cunningham once said. "I said that when I came here, not when I got this job."

Gunther Cunningham twice served as Chiefs defensive coordinator and was the team's head coach for two seasons. Cunningham was regarded as a brilliant defensive coordinator and his aggressive style was a perfect fit for the Chiefs. (Matt Brown/Icon Sportswire)

Cunningham often showed up for work at 4 a.m. and he had a close relationship with Derrick Thomas. Cunningham was Thomas' last head coach as the Kansas City icon and Pro Football Hall of Fame linebacker died in February 2000, a few weeks after being paralyzed from the chest down in a tragic car accident. The Chiefs entered the final week of the 1999 season with a 9-6 record and all they had to do was beat the Raiders at home to win the division and get a home playoff game. But the Chiefs blew a 17-point lead and lost 41-38 in overtime.

A few weeks later Thomas had that fateful car accident while driving too fast on an icy Interstate 435. Thomas' death affected everyone in the Chiefs community, but it probably affected Cunningham the most. Cunningham had just called Thomas from the Super Bowl a few days before, and Thomas was in good spirits and improving so his death came as a shock.

"Derrick said, 'Coach, be strong.' He never told me how strong I needed to be," an emotional Cunningham said during a press conference in Kansas City following Thomas' death.

Thomas' death hung over the team the following season, and the Chiefs finished 7-9. Cunningham was then fired, and for days he wouldn't get out of bed, completely crushed that he was let go from his beloved Chiefs.

Cunningham eventually picked himself up and went back to coaching, spending the next three seasons as an assistant with the Titans. Cunningham then returned to the Chiefs as defensive coordinator.

"This is about coaching players," Cunningham said then. "That's what I am, a football coach. I'm glad that I'm back. I missed this place and I missed these people."

While Cunningham coached the likes of Thomas, Neil Smith, Donnie Edwards and others in his first tenure with the Chiefs, during his second tenure he coached a young Derrick Johnson and Tamba Hali. After learning of Cunningham's death, Johnson paid his respects.

"Sad to hear about my coach Gunther Cunningham," he said. "He was my first D-coordinator for four years with the Chiefs. He helped me create a strong foundation that lasted 10 years after coaching me. My prayers go out to his wife and family."

Chiefs-turned-Raiders quarterback Rich Gannon also paid his respects on Twitter.

"Sad to hear of the passing of one of the best coaches in the game, Gunther Cunningham," Gannon said. "I went against him and his defense in practice every day for four years with KC and it definitely made me a better player. He was intense and took it personally if you had any success vs. his unit!"

Cunningham finished his coaching career serving eight seasons with the Lions before retiring and joining Pro Football Focus in 2017.

"My family and I are deeply saddened to hear the news of Gunther's passing," said Chiefs owner Clark Hunt. "During his nine seasons as defensive coordinator and two as head coach of the Kansas City Chiefs, he led some of the most feared defenses in our franchise's history with his energetic and motivating coaching style. Gunther made a tremendous impact on so many lives on and off the playing field in nearly five decades of coaching. Our heartfelt condolences go out to René, Natalie, Adam and the entire Cunningham family during this difficult time."

Dick Vermeil

Throughout his tenure as Chiefs general manager, Carl Peterson called his close friend Dick Vermeil once a week. After the 2000 season ended those conversations took on a different tone.

The Chiefs had just finished up a disappointing 7-9 season under second-year head coach Gunther Cunningham. Peterson wasn't necessarily unhappy with Cunningham—who had gone 9-7 the year before when he replaced Marty Schottenheimer—it was the thought that he could finally convince Vermeil to coach the Chiefs.

Cunningham had been a loyal soldier to the Chiefs since he arrived in 1995, coaching linebackers and serving as defensive coordinator. Peterson also knew Cunningham long before he came to the Chiefs so cutting ties with him would be tough to do. But during the season, Peterson sensed that Vermeil missed coaching and thought he might want to get back in the game.

A year earlier, Vermeil coached the St. Louis Rams to a Super Bowl title then went out on top. That marked the second time in Vermeil's career that he walked away from the game. He took the 1980 Eagles to the Super Bowl, but stepped down two years later because of burnout.

Vermeil spent the next 14 years as a football analyst before agreeing to coach the Rams in 1997. When Peterson called Vermeil, Redskins owner Dan Snyder was already at Vermeil's house in Philadelphia trying to convince him to come out of retirement. A couple days later, Peterson and vice president of operations Lynn Stiles flew to Philly to meet with Vermeil to try to do the same.

"I told him he was spinning his wheels," Vermeil said of Peterson's recruitment efforts.

Peterson didn't give in, and the morning after their meeting, Vermeil called to let him know he would be the next coach of the Chiefs. Peterson actually offered the job to Vermeil before he hired Schottenheimer in 1989, but Vermeil wasn't ready to return to the sidelines.

With Vermeil in tow, he brought over Al Saunders to be the team's offensive coordinator. The next step was finding a quarterback who could run the "Greatest Show on Turf" on the grass field at Arrowhead Stadium.

The Chiefs eventually acquired Trent Green in a trade with the Rams, and with Priest Holmes, Tony Gonzalez, Will Shields, Willie Roaf and Brian Waters, they had the personnel to run Vermeil's desired offense. The defense, however, leaked like a sieve.

In the 12 seasons prior to Vermeil's arrival, the Chiefs defense ranked third in points allowed (18.1) and fourth in sacks (522). Vermeil's defenses under Greg Robinson didn't come close to putting up those numbers, and in 2003 the defensive woes came to a head in the playoffs against Peyton Manning and the Colts when neither team punted and the Chiefs lost 38-31.

The day after the game, Robinson met with Vermeil and offered to resign. Vermeil thought about it for a day and agreed it would be best. Ironically, Robinson's replacement was Cunningham, who spent the previous three seasons with the Titans after being fired from the Chiefs.

The Chiefs went 10-6 in 2005 but missed the playoffs. The day before the last game of the season, Vermeil walked into Peterson's office and told him it was time.

Vermeil, who was an emotional coach, got a teary-eyed sendoff from his players as the Chiefs routed the Bengals 37-3 at Arrowhead. In five seasons at the helm, Vermeil went 44-36.

Since leaving the game, Vermeil has run a successful wine business in his home state of California. And in 2013, he helped the Chiefs land a pretty sweet deal when they were looking for a new coach.

Andy Reid

A coach's playbook can easily be more than 200 pages in length. This football Bible contains not only drawings of X's and O's but principles and strategies designed to help one succeed on the football field and in the game of life.

Hard work, setting goals, reaching goals, and having fun along the way are such big parts of what makes life enjoyable. Similarly, football is also largely about finding solutions to whatever problem you're faced with at that particular moment, and persevering if you fall short.

In the last 20 years, no one in the NFL has exemplified this more than Chiefs coach Andy Reid. Hired by Clark Hunt six years ago, Reid has led a revival of the franchise and taken it within one play of dethroning a dynasty and playing in the Super Bowl.

Even in the toughest of defeats, like the Chiefs' 37-31 loss to the Patriots in the 2019 AFC championship game, Reid can see what may yet be for his team in 2019 and beyond.

"There's a lot of things to be optimistic about," Reid said. "I've just got to get through. You've got to give me a little more time."

Reid is in his early 60s, but with Patrick Mahomes at quarterback he may have a long career ahead of him yet. Reid, who grew up near the bright lights of Hollywood, has devoted most of his life to football. He has gone from being an assistant to taking a team to the Super Bowl only to be fired years later. Reid, though, has made quite a comeback and is now the most influential coach in the game.

The Chiefs have enjoyed a resurgence since Andy Reid became coach in 2013. The Chiefs have won the last three AFC West titles and last year made the AFC championship game for the first time in 25 years. (Todd Kirkland/Icon Sportswire)

Coast to Coast

The son of Walter and Elizabeth, Reid grew up in Los Angeles on Holly Knoll Drive, just a mile away from Hollywood Boulevard. His father got a job working at Disney and later created scenic backgrounds and props for various TV, film and stage productions, including "Annie Get Your Gun."

As a kid, Reid helped cater events for the Tonight Show with Johnny Carson. There he saw the likes of John Wayne and Wilt Chamberlain. Big for his age, Reid always loved sports. At 13, he competed in the NFL's Punt, Pass and Kick contest on Monday Night Football.

In the now-famous YouTube clip, Reid looks more like a grown man compared to the other kids standing behind him in line. In fact, Reid was so big for his age that attendants had to go to the Rams locker room to find a jersey big enough to fit him.

Reid also worked as a vendor at Dodger Stadium and attended John Marshall High School, the same school as Leonardo DiCaprio. Skilled in carpentry and welding, Reid could have made a living doing a number of things. As a student at BYU, where he played tackle and guard protecting Jim McMahon, Reid entertained the thought of becoming a sportswriter and even wrote columns for the school newspaper.

Reid instead earned his bachelor's degree in physical education before earning his master's. In grad school, he became an assistant on the football team. Working alongside Hall of Famer LaVell Edwards, coaching became Reid's passion.

For the next 10 years, Reid coached the offensive line at San Francisco State, Northern Arizona, UTEP and Missouri before joining Mike Holmgren's staff as an offensive assistant with the Packers in 1992, the same year they acquired Brett Favre. The West Coast offense has been the foundation of Reid's offensive system ever since as he worked for Holmgren for seven seasons coaching the offensive line, quarterbacks and tight ends.

Holmgren, of course, had previously served on Bill Walsh's staff with the 49ers, coaching quarterbacks Joe Montana and Steve Young before becoming offensive coordinator and later head coach of the Packers.

"I'm a big Mike Holmgren fan," Reid said. "Obviously I felt at the time I had a hard time believing anybody did it better, and I've been a head coach for all these years, and I still feel that way. I just think he was unbelievable."

Reid earned a Super Bowl ring with the Packers when they defeated the Patriots in Super Bowl XXXI. In 1999, the Eagles named him their new coach despite him having no head coaching experience and technically no experience as a coordinator. At the time, Reid's hiring was met with a slew of criticism from fans and media. One columnist for the Philadelphia Inquirer wrote that "we want a who's who and you give us a who's he."

Reid, though, earned their praise. His first season with the Eagles, Reid drafted quarterback Donovan McNabb and led the team to a 5-11 record—a two-win improvement from the previous year. Reid started that season with veteran Doug Pederson at quarterback, but McNabb took over late in the year. By 2000, the Eagles were flying once again.

Reid guided the team to five straight playoff appearances. The 2004 team went to the Super Bowl but lost to Tom Brady and Bill Belichick by a field goal. Reid's teams went to the playoffs nine times and played in five NFC championship games in his 14 seasons in Philly, but he was fired after going 4-12 in 2012. Reid left Philly as the Eagles' all-time leader in wins with 130 and the most playoff wins with 10.

'Big Red'

It's an appropriate nickname for the coach, who stands 6-foot-3 and is always decked out in red along the Chiefs sideline. But the nickname itself predates Reid's arrival in Kansas City, a time when his hair really was that color.

After Reid was let go in Philadelphia, many believed he would sit out the 2013 season, wore down from the way things ended with the Eagles, and more seriously the death of his son.

Garrett, who was Reid's oldest son, died of a heroin overdose during training camp in 2012. He was just 29. Though Reid and his family were still mourning the loss of a loved one, the NFL kept calling.

The first call Reid took that Monday was from Hunt, whose Chiefs had just wrapped up a 2-14 season. The Chargers and Cardinals also contacted Reid, who also told them that he would not sit the season out.

"This is what I do," Reid said. "Never took that into consideration."

Hunt and Reid scheduled an interview for Wednesday at a Philadelphia airport, and the meeting lasted more than nine hours. Hunt, though, knew early on that he wanted Reid to be his new coach. Likewise, Reid wanted to go to Kansas City but first placed a call to Dick Vermeil, whom he had known for years.

Reid asked him if he should take the job, and Vermeil enthusiastically said yes. Reid canceled scheduled meetings with the Chargers and Cardinals and became the Chiefs coach on Jan. 4, 2013. Throughout the hiring process, Hunt also talked to Marty Schottenheimer. The former Chiefs coach was thrilled when he heard Reid was a Chief.

"He's got a hell of a lot of work to do," Schottenheimer told USA Today after Reid's hiring. "At the end of the day it all comes down to your ability to be trustworthy and be able to address issues in a controlled, frank way. I'm excited for the Chiefs."

At his introductory news conference in Kansas City, Reid provided few details—something that hasn't changed much over the years. But he was steadfast in one regard—finding the next quarterback.

"I've got to find the next Len Dawson, doggone it," he said.

'How 'bout those Chiefs!?'

Though Reid isn't very revealing when dealing with the press, he does have a good sense of humor and often jokes about his love for burgers and steaks with the media and his players, who admire him greatly.

After every Chiefs win, Reid will walk into the locker room and begin his postgame speech by saying, "How 'bout those Chiefs!?" It always evokes a big roar from the team, and Reid also has been known to dab on occasion.

In six seasons with the Chiefs, Reid has led the team to the playoffs five times and compiled a 65-31 record in the regular season, and his 67.7 winning percentage is the best of any Chiefs coach. In 2018, Reid also passed Schottenheimer for seventh on the NFL's all-time wins list with 207, including postseason.

Reid's coaching tree also is impressive. In 2018 he had seven former assistants working as head coaches. Among them, Jim Harbaugh (Ravens) and Pederson (Eagles) have won Super Bowls as head coaches and Ron Rivera (Panthers) took his team to one.

Also, Matt Nagy, Reid's former quarterbacks coach and offensive coordinator with the Chiefs, coached the Bears to the playoffs in his first season at the helm after learning from one of the best.

"There's never panic with Coach (Reid)," Nagy said. "That's a calm for everybody, players and coaches. And when you have that calm, you stick together, and you focus on yourself, and usually when that happens good things occur."

Reid's newest protégé is Eric Bieniemy. The former Colorado star played running back for Reid in 1999 and later joined his Chiefs staff in 2013. Bieniemy coached running backs for five seasons before being promoted to offensive coordinator when Nagy left for Chicago. In 2018, the Chiefs led the NFL in scoring, and Bieniemy's profile increased significantly.

"Coach Reid puts a lot of heat on me, but in a good way because why?" Bieniemy said. "I have to be ready. Just like when we're applying pressure on these guys to get ready, he's applying that same pressure. But also there is a comfort level to it because obviously he has expectations for me."

Bieniemy interviewed for a few head coaching positions in January for the 2019 season but wasn't hired. However, he appears to be the next big branch coming from Reid's tree.

"I'm a big fan of his," Reid said. "I think he'd be phenomenal."

Pat on the back

Most coaches wouldn't want their quarterback to throw the ball with his opposite hand while an All-Pro linebacker is bearing down on him along the sideline, nor would they want him to make no-look passes against one of the league's top defenses. But Reid isn't most coaches. If anything, he's the perfect coach for Mahomes, who often stops by his office early in the morning before practice.

"I go in there and draw up some plays, and he's like, 'I already thought of that,'" Mahomes said. "But I like that. He is as competitive as anyone is, and he's going to make sure he's ready for anything and make sure I am as well."

That includes dealing with the media. Mahomes typically meets with reporters twice a week during the season, once before practice and after the game. Reid has noticed that Mahomes has helped make for some good copy.

"Some of you guys he's made a better writer out of," Reid joked.

In his first year as a starter, Mahomes couldn't have played much better as he and Reid nearly took the Chiefs to the Super Bowl. Now Reid plans on getting another shot at it very soon.

"We were this close—an offside—to being in Atlanta," Reid said. "I'm going to work like crazy on my end to make sure it's right while keeping in mind of doing everything I think is right for the Chiefs.

"It's not easy to be in the (AFC) championship game. This isn't an easy thing. There's a lot of credit that goes out to these guys that busted their tail to put this organization and this city to have an opportunity like that. That's a special thing. We'll take care of that."

CHAPTER 5
QUARTERBACKS

Len Dawson

Football players dream of getting that first call to the NFL. Len Dawson was just hoping for a chance to continue his career. Well, more accurately, he was hoping to finally get it started.

In 1962, Dawson was 27 and looking for work. One day he got a call from an old acquaintance—his former assistant coach at Purdue—Hank Stram.

"How are you doing?" Stram asked.

"I'm not doing worth a damn," Dawson replied.

Dawson had good reason to be down in the dumps. He was selected fifth overall in the first round by the Steelers in 1957 and spent his first three seasons in the league on the bench. That number increased to five when he toiled away for two more years as a member of the Cleveland Browns.

The Browns acquired Dawson from the Steelers in a trade on Dec. 1, 1959, believing he could fill the gaping hole at quarterback that had plagued the franchise since Otto Graham retired in 1955. The Browns were quite high on Dawson dating back to the draft and they were even a little upset when the Steelers picked him one spot ahead of them on draft day.

Missing out on Dawson, Cleveland selected Syracuse running back Jim Brown with the next pick and somehow made do in the backfield for the next nine years.

Kansas City quarterback Len Dawson looks to pass against the New York Jets on Nov. 7, 1971, in New York. Dawson is the Chiefs' all-time leading passer and was MVP of Super Bowl IV. He also was inducted into the Pro Football Hall of Fame both as a player and broadcaster. (Kenneth Spencer Research Library, University of Kansas Libraries)

In his first five NFL seasons, Dawson started just two games and completed a grand total of 21 passes for 204 yards with three touchdowns and five interceptions. Not exactly gaudy numbers for someone who led the Big Ten in passing three straight years and was Purdue's all-time leading passer when his college career ended.

"I was the No. 1 draft pick of the Pittsburgh Steelers and for two or three years I didn't get to play anything," Dawson said. "Then I went to the Cleveland Browns for two or three years and didn't do anything there. So (Stram) said whenever you get free, let me know because I'd like to have you on my team.

"So I went to Paul Brown in Cleveland and asked him to put me on waivers. I might have been the first person to ever do that in the history of professional football. And he did. And I passed through. Of course, he did it in June when everybody on the coaching staff took time off back in those days. And a lot of them didn't know that I was on waivers."

After Brown granted Dawson his release, he felt he had to call Stram and give him the bad news. Dawson's skills had diminished greatly since Stram last coached him at Purdue. His footspeed and velocity on his passes were much slower and the tight spiral was gone.

Brown also said Dawson had a bad attitude, but five years of sitting on the bench can do that. Being reunited with Stram, Dawson eventually shook off the rust and bad habits and became the quarterback Stram envisioned when he watched him play in high school.

"So I got an opportunity to go to Texas," Dawson said. "And we won the championship that year, and then Lamar Hunt wasn't going to fight for two teams in Dallas, Texas. So he was going to move the franchise and he was going to move it to Kansas City, Mo. And I talked to Hank, and I wanted to know where training camp was going to be because Dallas, Texas, in July and August, it's unbearable. I'm telling you!

"And he said, 'Leonard,' with his sense of humor, 'you'll be happy to know we're moving north.' He didn't tell me it was 15 minutes north of downtown Kansas City, Mo."

Seventh son of a seventh son

Born to James and Annie Dawson on June 20, 1935, in Alliance, Ohio, Leonard Ray Dawson was the ninth of 11 children. He also happened to be the seventh son of a seventh son.

"I don't know what that means," Dawson said with a grin. "It means you get a lot of clothes from your older brothers. But I learned a lot of lessons. One is hard work and to treat people right."

In high school, he played football, basketball and baseball, but excelled on the gridiron and basketball court. His older brothers taught him how to play sports and he was recruited by Ohio State. But even with strong Ohio roots, Dawson chose to go to Purdue mainly because of his close relationship with Stram.

In college and the NFL, Dawson wore No. 16. And yes, the number has significance as one plus six equals seven. And being the seventh son of a seventh son, Dawson always thought that brought him good luck.

At 6-feet tall and 190 pounds, Dawson was undersized even for his era. But his mobility and accuracy allowed him to flourish in Stram's offensive system that featured plenty of rollouts designed to open passing lanes for his quarterback.

During his 14 seasons with the Texans/Chiefs, Dawson was elected to the Pro Bowl seven times. He led the NFL in completion percentage seven times, passer rating six times and touchdowns four times. He also called most of the plays.

Lenny the Cool

Besides being a skilled play-caller, one of Dawson's greatest strengths was that he never got rattled no matter the situation. With this in mind, his teammates gave him the nickname "Lenny the Cool."

Dawson's calm, cool and collected demeanor, however, was tested during the 1969 season. He suffered a torn MCL in his left knee in Week 2. In today's game, a torn MCL might keep a player sidelined for eight or 10 weeks. But back then an MCL injury would require season-ending surgery, something Dawson and the Chiefs desperately wanted to avoid.

For a while that seemed inevitable. In the days that followed, Stram had five different doctors examine Dawson's knee. They all determined surgery was the only option. Four of the doctors were in Oklahoma City, and Dawson was even prepped for surgery once.

But a sixth physician—Dr. Frank Reynolds of St. Louis—believed Dawson's knee could be healed without surgery and he could return in six weeks if he stayed on crutches for three weeks and underwent vigorous rehab for three weeks. Dawson and the Chiefs went that route and he only missed five games.

In his return against the Buffalo Bills, Dawson completed just 7 of 14 passes for 94 yards, but the Chiefs rallied with 23 points in the fourth quarter as Jan Stenerud kicked three field goals and Mike Garrett scored two touchdowns to lead the Chiefs to a 29-7 win.

The next week against San Diego, Dawson threw three picks, but the Chiefs won 27-3. The following week, Dawson threw three touchdowns in a 34-16 road win against Joe Namath and the Jets. Dawson played with a heavy heart as his father died in his sleep two days before. Dawson, though, completed 23 of 38 passes for 285 yards.

In a rematch against the Jets in the playoffs, Dawson completed just 12 of 27 passes but a 19-yard touchdown pass in the fourth quarter gave the Chiefs a 13-6 win. The next game against Oakland, the Chiefs trailed 7-0 after the first quarter but scored 17 unanswered to win.

Dawson completed just 7 of 17 passes but fueled by rushing touchdowns from Mike Garrett and Wendell Hayes and a dominating defense that picked off four passes, the Chiefs advanced to face the Vikings in the Super Bowl.

On the game's biggest stage, Dawson played brilliantly. He completed 12 of 17 passes for 142 yards and his 43-yard touchdown pass to Otis Taylor in the third quarter sealed the Chiefs' 23-7 win. Dawson was named the game's MVP, but he credited the defense for becoming world champions.

"I had such great teammates," he said. "Teammates that wanted to play and wanted to win. I remember Super Bowl IV against Minnesota, I knew that we were going to have an easy time because I looked at our defense—and defense wins Super Bowls—and we had (six) guys out there who would be in the pro football Hall of Fame.

"They (the Vikings) didn't have a chance. All I had to do was not screw it up. That's what my teammates used to say. 'Goddamn it, Dawson, don't screw it up.' And I just relied on them and let them do all the hard work and I got all the glory," Dawson said with a laugh.

However, a week before the big game Dawson was in no mood to laugh. On NBC's nightly newscast, a report stated that Dawson was one of five football players who were to be subpoenaed the following week and called before a grand jury to testify in regards to an illegal gambling investigation.

At the center of it all was Donald "Dice" Dawson, a known bookmaker and gambler from Detroit. When he was arrested he had $400,000 on him as well as Len Dawson's phone number. Though the two were not related, they had met several years earlier, and Donald Dawson actually called the Chiefs quarterback a few times, including when he hurt his knee and after the death of his father.

In New Orleans with Stram at his side, Dawson held a news conference and said he only knew Donald Dawson from afar and didn't know anything about the investigation. The story soon died down after that and Dawson went about his business preparing for the game. He also never received a subpoena and didn't hear a word from the prosecutors in Detroit.

Dawson played six more seasons with the Chiefs and retired in 1975 as the team's all-time leader in completions (2,115), attempts (3,696), yards (28,507) and touchdowns (237). Dawson was elected to the Chiefs Hall of Fame in 1979 and the Pro Football Hall of Fame in 1987.

Another call to the Hall

While Dawson was the team's starting quarterback, he also doubled as a sportscaster on the nightly news—something that would never fly today.

Dawson began working at KMBC-TV in Kansas City in 1966 and thus became the first sports anchor in the town's history.

Back then the 10 p.m. news was only 15 minutes long and there was no sportscast. So Jack Steadman, the Chiefs GM, saw an opportunity. He called the station's general manager insisting that sports be part of the telecast, and he offered up his quarterback to do it.

The idea also was a publicity stunt for the Chiefs. Steadman believed that having the quarterback on TV might help sell tickets, but KMBC was skeptical at first.

"What kind of experience does he have?" Steadman was asked.

"Don't worry about it. He can handle it," Steadman replied, knowing Dawson had none.

During the season, Dawson was on the 10 p.m. news three nights a week. He was a natural in front of the camera and from 1976 to 1984 he worked for NBC as a color analyst for NFL games. In 1977 executives in New York asked Dawson to join a startup show called Inside the NFL on HBO. Dawson received permission from KMBC to do the show as cable was new and not considered competition for a local TV station at that time.

When the show first started, the Missouri side of Kansas City didn't have cable so Dawson had to go to a friend's house on the Kansas side to watch it.

In 1984, Dawson joined the Chiefs radio network as a commentator and served in that capacity until 2016. In 2017, he scaled back his duties, doing pregame work before retiring from broadcasting altogether at the end of the season. On Oct. 30, 2017, the Chiefs renamed their broadcast booth in his honor.

"It has been a privilege to be side by side with him for 24 years because he was a boyhood hero of mine," said Mitch Holthus, the voice of the Chiefs since 1994. "He really redefined this whole city and the region. The A's were here, but they weren't any good, and they wanted to move. Then when Lamar moved the Dallas Texans here and they became the Kansas City Chiefs, the Chiefs were on the national map starting with that run to get to Super Bowl I and to win Super Bowl IV.

"It's easy to lose track of what an incredible career he's had as a broadcaster because he was such a great player. And it's easy to lose track of what a great player he was because he's such a great broadcaster."

Dawson was elected to the Pro Football Hall of Fame as a broadcaster in 2012, becoming just the third person in history to accomplish that feat, joining Frank Gifford and Dan Dierdorff.

"Next to my father, Lamar, few people have had a greater impact on this franchise than Len Dawson," Chiefs owner Clark Hunt said. "Over the course of his legendary career—first as a player then as a broadcaster—Len has been a part of every major moment in Chiefs history. On the field and behind the camera 'Lenny the Cool' has always been at the center of the action. And he has represented the Chiefs and Kansas City with tremendous class for more than 55 years."

Joe Montana

Back on the field at Arrowhead Stadium, with a Sea of Red around him, Joe Montana waves his red and gold Chiefs scarf to pump up the home crowd.

It's the first half of the 2019 AFC championship game between the Patriots and Chiefs, and Montana is standing in the corner of the end zone yelling, "Let's go!" as the crowd roars at the sight of the NFL icon.

Twenty-five years earlier, Montana quarterbacked the Chiefs to the AFC title game. Memories of that frigid day in Buffalo are foggy for him because he was knocked out early in the second half and spent the rest of the afternoon sitting on the sideline watching the Bills roll to another Super Bowl.

Joe Montana played just two seasons for the Chiefs but took the 1993 team to the AFC title game. Here he is throwing a pass against the Cleveland Browns on Nov. 20, 1994, at Arrowhead Stadium. (John Cordes/Icon Sportswire)

Montana had hoped these Chiefs could take that last step, the step his teams were never able to make during his two seasons in Kansas City. But Tom Brady's bunch outlasted Patrick Mahomes and the Chiefs 37-31 in an overtime thriller that turned heartbreaker for the Chiefs.

Montana's wife, Jennifer, was at the game, too, wearing his replica Chiefs jersey. And being on the field brought back the sort of rush he used to get when he would drive his team to a win.

"Adrenaline still racing from being back on the sidelines with my beautiful wife at Arrowhead," Montana tweeted after the game. "Thanks for having us @Chiefs! Hats off to two absolute superstars and their teams @patrickmahomes5 and @TB12sports...And the gunslinger in the booth @tonyromo – Incredible game!"

Winning playoff games is what Montana did best. His four Super Bowl rings with the San Francisco 49ers tied Pittsburgh's Terry Bradshaw for the most by a quarterback in NFL history until Brady passed them with his fifth in 2017.

Montana, arguably the greatest quarterback of all time, hoped to get a fifth Super Bowl ring with the 49ers but age and injuries took their toll on the three-time Super Bowl MVP and he was deemed expendable following the 1992 season in favor of Steve Young.

Montana, though, wanted to keep playing and several teams were interested. But Kansas City would become his home for the next two years. And by the time he returned to San Francisco, he left behind a highlight reel of memories that remain vivid today.

A KC comeback

Coming off a 17-0 loss to San Diego in the playoffs, the Chiefs were in need of an offensive overhaul. The decision was made by Marty Schottenheimer to drop the smash-mouth football he had become known for and replace it with Bill Walsh's West Coast offense.

Schottenheimer hired Paul Hackett, who had coached quarterbacks and receivers with the 49ers, as offensive coordinator and things were starting to take shape early in the 1993 calendar year. The only problem was they needed a quarterback to run the offense.

The Chiefs felt they had a quality quarterback with Dave Krieg but knew it would take time for him to get comfortable in the new offense—his third in three years. So the Chiefs huddled up and talked about other possibilities and quickly zeroed in on the Bay Area.

In 1991, Montana suffered a torn flexor tendon in his right elbow in training camp and underwent season-ending surgery that October. He returned in 1992 and appeared in the last game of the regular season, playing the second half.

Young started all 16 games that season and the playoffs. He and Montana actually were pretty good friends at one time. They played golf together, and Montana even had Young over for Christmas dinner one year. But Montana and Young were always rivals on the field, and the 49ers weren't about to let a quarterback controversy continue for a seventh season.

Lynn Stiles, who was vice president of player personnel for the Chiefs at the time, also had been an assistant with San Francisco prior to joining the Chiefs. Stiles still had connections to the 49ers and he knew the soon-to-be 37-year-old Montana would be the one on the trading block. But before that could happen, the 49ers first had to take care of some quarterback housekeeping.

Young and Steven Bono's contracts were both up, and the 49ers placed the franchise tag on Young. The Chiefs were in the process of signing Bono, who made a free-agent visit to Kansas City, but the 49ers re-signed him before a deal with the Chiefs was finalized.

With Young and Bono under contract, the 49ers could move forward in trading Montana. The thought of adding him to the roster excited the Chiefs, who believed a Super Bowl might be closer than they thought. So Carl Peterson picked up the phone and called 49ers president Carmen Policy.

The 49ers initially wanted the Chiefs' first-, second- and third-round picks, which Peterson thought was outrageous. With Montana officially on the market, though, the 49ers let him shop his services to other teams. The Chiefs and Cardinals were Montana's two finalists, with each team getting two visits.

The Chiefs hosted Montana first, as he flew in on April 7, 1993. The next day, he flew to Phoenix and met with the Cardinals. A week later, Montana and his wife returned to Kansas City, and the Chiefs put on a full-court press, wining and dining on the Plaza and showing Jennifer the neighborhood where the Montana children would attend school.

Later that Friday night at dinner, Peterson and Montana's agent agreed to a new three-year contract that would pay him $10 million. Montana then proposed a toast to Chiefs owner Lamar Hunt, and to a fifth Super Bowl ring for his right hand. But Montana to the Chiefs wasn't yet a done deal.

On Saturday, the 49ers sent a private plane to Kansas City, and the Montana's boarded it. First stop was Youngstown, Ohio, to meet with 49ers owner Eddie DeBartolo, who had an important message from head coach George Siefert.

DeBartolo said Siefert had changed his mind and Montana would now be the team's "designated starter" entering training camp. Montana and DeBartolo returned to San Francisco on Sunday and the 49ers again made their pitch to Montana that he would be the starter.

After watching Young play for the last two seasons, and being named league MVP, Montana didn't believe what he was hearing. A day later, he told the 49ers that he wanted to play for the Chiefs and released a statement.

"I was told in January that Steve Young would be the starter, and I accepted the 49ers' position," Montana said. "Due to this decision, the 49ers authorized me to work out an arrangement with another NFL team. Three days prior to my decision to go with the Kansas City Chiefs, once again the 49ers stated publicly there would be no open competition for the starting job.

"Although Mr. DeBartolo and I spoke on Saturday about finishing my career with the 49ers, it is not going to be possible based on the commitment I made to the Chiefs on Friday. It is in my interests, and that of my family, to play for the Kansas City Chiefs."

The deal took a couple days to complete, and on April 21, 1993, Montana's days in a 49ers uniform were over. The Chiefs sent their first-round pick—18th overall—in the 1993 draft to the 49ers for safety David Whitmore and a third-round selection in the 1994 draft.

In San Francisco, tears flooded the Bay Area. In Kansas City, fans rejoiced with Super Bowl dreams.

Joe Cool

When the team bus arrived in River Falls, Wis., to start training camp, Montana Mania had spread everywhere. There was even a huge billboard that read, "Welcome Joe Montana and the Kansas City Chiefs."

On the first day of camp, hundreds gathered to try and catch a glimpse of Montana. By the time the Chiefs held their first scrimmage, 9,000 fans crammed in around the field to watch Montana play. Some of them made the drive all the way from San Francisco.

Increased security made it a little tougher to get around, but Montana was gracious with his time, signing autographs and taking pictures with fans often during his time with the Chiefs.

Montana's roommate at training camp and on the road was Krieg. Hoping to avoid some of the issues he had with Young in San Francisco, Montana made a point to hang out with him often. Krieg, who grew up in Wisconsin, also had family in the area. He and Montana played golf regularly, ate at Steve's Pizza and went on beer runs together at night.

Montana also brought a wave of new business to Kansas City. He started a beer distribution company, and whenever he was at a restaurant word traveled fast. Within minutes the place would be filled to capacity.

Chiefs merchandise sales rose to near the top of the league, and demand for tickets reached an all-time high. So, too, was Montana's drive to get back on the field. The only question was could he still play. The answer was a resounding yes.

Montana Magic

Montana wore No. 16 with the 49ers, but the Chiefs had already retired that number in honor of Len Dawson. So Montana picked No. 19—the number he wore as a kid playing Pop Warner football—to be his last.

In 1993, the Chiefs opened the preseason at Green Bay, but they elected to sit Montana. The next week, the Chiefs were set to play the Bills at Arrowhead, and Montana would make his debut in a Chiefs uniform. The game was broadcast on TNT, and when Montana ran from the tunnel onto the field for the first time, the thunderous ovation even caught him by surprise.

"I don't think words can describe the good feeling you get from that," Montana said after the game. "It's something I won't forget."

A few weeks later on Sept. 5, 1993, he made his regular-season debut at Tampa Bay. Montana came out firing, completing his first nine passes en route to a 246-yard, three-touchdown performance in the Chiefs' 27-3 win.

Montana displayed everything coaches wanted to see out of a West Coast offense quarterback. He threw short, deep and connected with second or third receivers. Montana's first two touchdown passes came on a 19-yard strike to

Willie Davis and a 50-yarder to J.J. Birden. His third came on a 12-yard pass to Marcus Allen a play after he bruised his wrist.

Montana missed the following game against the Oilers with a sore wrist before returning for the home opener against the Broncos on Monday Night Football. The Chiefs won 15-7 on five Nick Lowery field goals.

"It was our first big national TV game against John Elway and the Broncos, two really good teams," Lowery said. "And it's Joe vs. John, and in that game we score zero touchdowns, but somebody kicked five field goals. And Huey Lewis was on the sidelines and he was standing right next to the field goal net.

"So I hit a 52-yarder, and a 44-yarder, and I kept going back. I had four in the first half. And he was like, 'Man, this is easy for you.' And it was so cool because I'm standing there next to Huey Lewis for most of the first half, and as he's watching me at the net I'd run onto the field, kick a field goal and come back. That was pretty cool. And on the front page of USA Today, it's not a picture of Joe. It's a picture of me. And he, of course, gave me shit afterwards because he wasn't used to the kicker getting more publicity than he did."

The Chiefs finished the regular season with an 11-5 record and won the AFC West title for the first time since 1971.

"Joe was this star," Lowery said. "I knew he did great in the games, and I knew he did extra great in the big games, like he did in the second half and in the fourth quarter against Pittsburgh in that playoff game. But a really important thing to share is that he also was deadly accurate in practice.

"It was like watching a conductor of the Metropolitan Opera, just the precision. Every pass, it wasn't just hitting the guy, it was perfectly in step. And one of the great lessons you hear is practice makes perfect. But perfect practice makes perfect. So you can say that a Tom Brady or a Joe Montana or a Drew Brees or a Patrick Mahomes or whoever, great quarterbacks are usually great in the games and it's because they're great in practice. They understand and love the work and the preparation and the focus."

In 1993, Montana went 8-3 as a starter, completed 60 percent of his passes and threw 13 touchdowns. Despite missing five games with injuries, he was elected to the Pro Bowl.

In the playoffs, Montana shined as well. In the Wild Card game against the Steelers, the Chiefs faced a fourth-and-goal from the 7 with 1:48 to play, but Montana found Tim Barnett in the back of the end zone for the tying score. The Chiefs went on to win 27-24 in overtime on a Lowery 32-yard field goal.

The following week at Houston, Montana threw for 299 yards and three touchdowns, including a 7-yard strike to Keith Cash in the third quarter. Cash spiked the ball against a poster of Oilers defensive coordinator Buddy Ryan, sparking the Chiefs' 28-20 win in a game they trailed 10-0 at halftime.

In the AFC championship game at Buffalo, the Chiefs lost 30-13. The outcome might have been different had Montana not gotten a concussion early in the second half.

In 1994, the Chiefs went 9-7 as Montana played in 14 games, going 9-5 as a starter. Two of those wins came in a couple of the most memorable games in team history. In Week 2, Montana faced Young and the 49ers at Arrowhead Stadium.

Montana completed 19 of 31 passes for 203 yards and two touchdowns in the Chiefs' 24-17 victory. Young, meanwhile, went 24 of 34 for 288 yards with a touchdown and two picks. He also was sacked four times.

On Oct. 17, 1994, on Monday Night Football, Montana engineered the Mile High Miracle. He drove the Chiefs 75 yards in nine plays, capped off by a 5-yard touchdown pass to Willie Davis at the right front pylon with eight seconds remaining to give the Chiefs a thrilling 31-28 win. Montana completed 34 of 54 passes for 393 yards and three touchdowns that night.

In 1994, Montana completed 60 percent of his passes, threw for 3,283 yards and 16 touchdowns to go with nine interceptions. The Chiefs traveled to Miami to face Dan Marino and the Dolphins in the first round and led 14-7 at the end of the first quarter on two Montana touchdowns. But the Dolphins rallied for a 27-17 win, ending the Chiefs' season.

Though Montana had a year remaining on his contract, he decided to call it a career at age 38. In two magical seasons with the Chiefs, Montana threw for 5,427 yards to go with 29 touchdowns and 16 interceptions. He went 17-8 as a starter, won two playoff games and gave Chiefs fans plenty of reason to wear his Chiefs jersey a quarter century later.

"It was truly a pleasure to be able to go from one great organization to another," Montana said when he formally announced his retirement in April 1995. "They took us in wholeheartedly and welcomed us, and we had a good time while we were there. And I thank them from the bottom of our heart, not only myself, but from my wife and kids."

Trent Green

When Dick Vermeil came out of retirement at age 64 to coach the Chiefs in January 2001, he already had a Pro-Bowl quarterback on the roster in Elvis Grbac.

Grbac had just thrown for 4,000 yards and 28 touchdowns in the 2000 season, and Vermeil was looking forward to working with him as his starting quarterback. That all changed a month later when Grbac's agent notified the Chiefs that he wanted out of Kansas City. Caught a bit off guard by Grbac's request, the Chiefs released him on March 1 and were without a quarterback for the next six weeks.

The team showed interest in several veterans in that time, including Trent Dilfer and Troy Aikman, but that was largely because the Chiefs and St. Louis Rams were playing a long game of poker for the services of Trent Green. Two years earlier at a dinner in downtown St. Louis, Vermeil convinced Green, a St. Louis native and free agent at the time, to sign with the Rams and be his quarterback.

The fact that Vermeil even made it to that dinner is pretty remarkable. On the drive over, Vermeil was running late and ran a red light and got hit by another car. Vermeil's car flipped over on its top, and he had to crawl out the passenger's side to get out. When Vermeil finally arrived for the meal, Green noticed the coach had bits of glass sticking in the skin on his hands. After Vermeil told him what happened, Green was so impressed that Vermeil still showed up, he immediately wanted to play for him.

Green didn't get much of a chance as he tore up his knee in a preseason game against the Chargers when Rodney Harrison went low and hit Green, tearing his ACL and MCL. Green was lost for the season and had to watch Kurt Warner guide Vermeil's team to the Super Bowl. In 2000, Green served as

Warner's backup and threw 16 touchdowns in eight games, showing he could play if he got an opportunity.

That came with the Chiefs when Carl Peterson finally agreed to send the Rams a first-round pick in exchange for Green. Over the next five and a half years, Green became the closest thing to a franchise quarterback the organization had seen since Len Dawson. With Green delivering the ball to Priest Holmes, Tony Gonzalez, Eddie Kennison and Dante Hall, the Chiefs broke pretty much every offensive record in team history at the time.

"It's a pick your poison thing with our offense," Green once said.

That also included right tackle John Tait. In the 2002 season opener at Cleveland, the Chiefs trailed the Browns 39-37 with three seconds to play when Green dropped back to pass. Cleveland linebacker Dwayne Rudd came flying in from the right side came and nearly pulled Green down.

For a second, Rudd actually believed he had sacked Green, and tossed his helmet in celebration thinking the game was over. But Green somehow managed to escape and lateraled the ball to Tait, who was behind him in the pocket. Tait took off down the left side line and rumbled 36 yards before being pushed out of bounds with all zeros on the clock.

Amidst the Browns' celebration, Rudd was flagged for unsportsmanlike conduct. Since a game cannot end on a defensive penalty, the Chiefs got to run another play. Morten Anderson then kicked a 30-yard field goal to give the Chiefs the win.

"They were rushing three and the linebacker was blitzing," Green said. "I was trying to buy time. He (Rudd) was spinning around, and I knew I was going down. John was the first guy I saw, and I knew it wasn't a forward pass. Instead of going down to the end of the game, I flipped it to big John to see what happens."

In 2003, Green led the Chiefs to a 13-3 record and the AFC West title, but the Chiefs couldn't get past Peyton Manning and the Colts in a playoff game that featured no punts. Vermeil retired in 2005, and Green's future with the club quickly took a drastic turn.

In the 2006 season opener against the Bengals, Green suffered a severe concussion when on a rollout he slid feet first, giving himself up to the defense. But as he went down, he took a hit to the helmet and his head bounced back hard on the field, knocking him out.

Green left the field on a stretcher and missed the next eight games. When he returned, the Chiefs went 4-3 the rest of the way and sneaked into the playoffs. But after another loss to the Colts, the organization wanted to go younger and give Brodie Croyle the reigns in 2007. Green was dealt to the Dolphins and his time with the Chiefs was over.

Green ranks second all-time in team passing yards (21,459), touchdowns (118), completions (1,720) and attempts (2,777), trailing only Dawson. Green started Miami's first five games in 2007 but another concussion—this time while trying to make a block—ended his season.

Green signed with the Rams the following year but played in only three games and retired that offseason to become a broadcaster. Green has served as color analyst on the Chiefs preseason TV broadcasts since 2010 and he joined CBS Sports in 2014. Green also has broadcast Thursday night games on the radio for Westwood One.

Alex Smith

Only a few players get better with age. Alex Smith was one of them as a member of the Chiefs. From 2013-17, Smith guided the Chiefs to a winning season each year and etched his name into the record books along the way.

His last year with the Chiefs was his best. At age 33, Smith threw for 4,042 yards with 26 touchdowns and just five interceptions. He also completed 67.5 percent of his passes and led the NFL in quarterback rating at 104.7.

But Smith, who carried a $17 million cap hit for the 2018 season, was traded to the Washington Redskins for cornerback Kendall Fuller and a third-round pick in the 2018 NFL Draft just weeks after the Chiefs suffered another heartbreaking home playoff loss to the Tennessee Titans.

In the hours after the trade, thousands of Chiefs fans showed their appreciation to Smith by donating $11—his jersey number—to the Alex Smith Foundation. Smith, who made the Pro Bowl three times with the Chiefs, finished his career third in completions (1,587), attempts (2,436), yards (17,608) and fourth in touchdowns (102). He also threw only 33 interceptions with the Chiefs.

"I know that stats are really popular, that people look into that stuff," Smith said. "But there's a lot of games where you walk out of and you feel great—and maybe you played lights-out—but the numbers didn't match it, but you did everything you could to help the team win. So I don't necessarily look at the stat line, but I think there's a lot more to it."

Smith posted a 50-26 record as a starter with the Chiefs after coming over in a trade with San Francisco for two second-round picks. Smith was never a superstar, but he was a solid performer who was modest and humble, which sufficed for most Chiefs fans.

Mobile and athletic, Smith also constantly watched film. His intellect gave him another weapon on game day, but he is always cautious in regards to his own success.

"I think you play long enough, you realize how quickly things can change," Smith said. "One week, everybody's raving about you, and how quickly it can flip if you drink the Kool-Aid. I think you've got to be careful with that."

Smith has always had good reason to feel that way. How could he not after playing for four head coaches and seven different offensive coordinators in his first seven seasons in the league? Smith played collegiately at Utah, and the 49ers selected him with the first overall pick in the 2005 draft.

He struggled mightily early in his career, throwing one touchdown and 11 interceptions as a rookie. He also felt the pressure of being a top pick and it showed in his play. However, Smith eventually had success with the 49ers and led them to the NFC title game in 2011.

Smith also got the 49ers off to a strong start in 2012 before a concussion forced him to the sideline. Colin Kaepernick took over and led the 49ers to the Super Bowl, and Smith was traded that offseason to Kansas City.

"Everybody's past is different," Smith said. "For me, coming in (to San Francisco), there were a lot of expectations and going through the process of dealing with those as a player is different for everybody.

"Certainly for me, it was tough early. It carried a lot of weight when I played and it took a while to shrug that off. It was a process. And I am not sure I would be where I am if I didn't go through it, as frustrating as it was."

A fresh start energized Smith, and playing for Andy Reid also gave his career a boost. When Smith came to town, he was much wiser having gone through a difficult situation in San Francisco and that made him appreciate the stability he had in Kansas City.

"I think it is just a different mindset of going and playing ball and not having the anxiety of that," Smith said. "And (having) the confidence in your teammates and yourself to just go out and play your game and to know that that is good enough."

Before Smith arrived, the Chiefs quarterbacks from 2007-12 were Brodie Croyle, Damon Huard, Tyler Thigpen, Tyler Palko, Matt Cassel, Kyle Orton and Brady Quinn. Not exactly a Joe Montana in that bunch, huh?

But Smith was somewhat Montana-like, as he led the Chiefs to their first playoff win in 22 years with a victory over the Houston Texans in January 2016. Smith guided the Chiefs to the playoffs in four of his five seasons and the team won the AFC West title in 2016 and 2017. Smith, however, played in just 10 games last season with the Redskins as a gruesome leg injury has put his career in jeopardy.

But for Reid, it was Smith's attention to detail, game day preparation and being a good teammate that set him apart.

"You all know what I think of him," Reid said.

During his first four seasons with the Chiefs, Smith routinely threw short passes, hitting receivers well in front of the sticks and only aired it out on rare occasion. But as the Chiefs assembled more weapons and speed around him, Smith evolved as a quarterback and became a deep-ball threat in 2017 when he led the NFL with 52 completions over 20 yards.

Smith also led the Chiefs in another way in 2017. He led the team to the division title and the playoffs and helped develop his replacement at the same time. Those are not easy tasks by themselves, but Smith handled it with class. Now the Chiefs—and Patrick Mahomes—are better for it.

Kansas City Chiefs quarterback Patrick Mahomes throws a 37-yard touchdown pass in the first quarter against the Arizona Cardinals on Nov. 11, 2018, at Arrowhead Stadium. The touchdown pass was Mahomes' 30th of the year, tying the franchise record set by Len Dawson. Mahomes broke Dawson's record later that day and finished with 50 touchdown passes in his first season as a starter. (Scott Winters/Icon Sportswire)

Patrick Mahomes

On April 27, 2017, the streak ended, and Chiefs fans finally got their wish. In a franchise-altering move, the Chiefs drafted Texas Tech quarterback Patrick Mahomes with the 10th pick in the first round of the NFL Draft.

For 34 long years, the team refused to draft a quarterback in the opening round. Burned by selecting Todd Blackledge seventh overall in 1983, the Chiefs passed on every opportunity to draft a quarterback in the first round until they traded up 17 spots and picked the kid with the big arm and off-the-charts potential.

Leading up to the draft, there wasn't much internal debate on which quarterback the Chiefs should take. North Carolina's Mitchell Trubisky was rated by most pundits as the top quarterback in the draft, and he would be long gone by the time the Chiefs picked. That left Clemson's Deshaun Watson, who had just led the Tigers to a win over Alabama in the NCAA title game, and Mahomes, who had wrapped up a 5-7 season with the Red Raiders.

On draft day, Trubisky was the first quarterback taken, going to the Bears second overall. Then, in a trade they had been working on for weeks with the Bills, the Chiefs played leapfrog and picked Mahomes, the second quarterback taken in that draft, but the one they felt had the highest ceiling of any player in the draft.

"We just thought with what we do, Mahomes would fit in well," Chiefs coach Andy Reid said. "We had all the guys in—all the quarterbacks came in. We had an opportunity to spend six hours with each guy. It was a great experience to meet all those guys. But we thought with what we do, Patrick would fit best."

Start of something special

When the Chiefs drafted Mahomes, John Dorsey was the general manager. By mid-July, he was out and Brett Veach was in. The top priority for both owner Clark Hunt and Veach was getting the quarterback of the future signed before training camp, and Mahomes wanted the same thing.

"I think with my agents and Mr. Hunt, they had good communication the whole way, and I knew that the contract was going to get done," Mahomes said. "I wanted to be at camp on time. I didn't want to miss any reps. I wanted to be here."

The minute the Chiefs drafted Mahomes, Alex Smith's days with the team were measured in mere months. In today's NFL, you don't move up 17 spots to let a guy sit on the bench for two seasons. So the Chiefs strategically placed Mahomes' locker next to Smith's, and told the veteran to look after him.

Early in his rookie year, Mahomes would show up at 6:30 for 7 a.m. film sessions. Smith, meanwhile, would already have been at the facility for at least an hour. Mahomes took note and eventually began showing up the same time as Smith.

The Chiefs wrapped up the division title with one game to go in the 2017 season. So Reid opted to give most of his starters the day off in the regular-season finale at Denver. That meant Smith would take a seat and prepare for the playoffs and Mahomes would get the call against the Broncos.

At that point, Mahomes hadn't played a single down. He played some in the preseason, but Smith had played every snap of the regular season. Even though Mahomes hadn't seen any real game action, Smith knew he was no ordinary rookie backup.

"He has a great ability to play the game and not get locked into schemes and fundamentals and things like that," Smith said just days before Mahomes'

Chiefs quarterback Patrick Mahomes reviews plays with coach Andy Reid as the Chiefs take on the San Francisco 49ers on Sept. 23, 2018, in Kansas City, Mo. (Robin Alam/Icon Sportswire)

first NFL start. "Those things are all important, don't get me wrong. But he has a great ability to go play and that's really important as well."

Though he threw an early pick, Mahomes settled down and wowed Chiefs fans with his arm, legs and Superman-like heroics against Denver's starters. Sparked by Mahomes, who fired a jaw-dropping 17-yard pass across the middle with a defender wrapped around his legs, the Chiefs' backups built a 24-10 lead in the fourth quarter. With a two-touchdown advantage, Reid gave Mahomes the rest of the day off—a reward for a job well done—and inserted third-stringer Tyler Bray.

Bray, however, fumbled the ball on his first snap, and Denver scooped it up and returned it 38 yards for a touchdown. The Chiefs then went three and out, and Denver promptly tied it with a touchdown.

With less than three minutes to go, Mahomes, who was on the sideline wearing a parka, was inserted back into the game by Reid. In the first two-minute drive of his career, he led the Chiefs on an 11-play drive that culminated with Harrison Butker's game-winning field goal as time expired.

Mahomes finished 22 of 35 for 284 yards with no touchdowns and a pick. More importantly, he reinforced the beliefs of the higher-ups that 2018 and beyond could be special with him at quarterback. A month later, the Chiefs dealt Smith to the Redskins, opening the door to a new era of Chiefs football.

Shooting star

Inside the team's training facility, there's a basketball goal in the locker room. A white stripe designates a makeshift free-throw line and a little bit beyond that there's a 3-point line.

One day, while me and the rest of the reporters waited on Smith for his weekly interview session, Mahomes walked out and put up a couple jumpers. Tyreek Hill and Mitchell Schwartz were his designated rebounders and, in this instance, so was I.

Mahomes' first shot bounced off the left side of the rim and rolled over to me. I was a good 15 feet away from the hoop and didn't have a clear lane to throw Mahomes the ball back. So with a pretty nifty bounce pass, I tossed it to Schwartz, who tossed it to Mahomes. His second shot was a near carbon copy of the first, and I remember thinking, "I'm glad he stuck with football," knowing full well the kid could hoop.

Mahomes played football, baseball and basketball at Whitehouse High in Whitehouse, Texas. He threw 50 touchdown passes his senior season and in the spring he threw a no-hitter for the baseball team. His riffle arm—which he estimates can throw a football 85 yards—is no doubt partly due to genetics. He is the son of Pat Mahomes Sr., a former Omaha Royals farmhand who pitched in the big leagues for 11 years.

The elder Mahomes spent parts of five seasons with the Twins and also played two years for the Red Sox and Mets before finishing his career with the Rangers, Cubs and Pirates. The younger Mahomes appeared in three games for the Red Raiders baseball team as a freshman and was considered a prospect.

The Tigers selected him in the 39th round of the 2014 draft, but Mahomes didn't sign as he ultimately chose to give up baseball and focus solely on football. Needless to say everyone in Chiefs Kingdom is super glad he did.

At Texas Tech, Mahomes wore No. 5, but that number was already taken when he became a Chief. So he chose No. 15 instead and it has been a hot commodity since.

"It still has the No. 5 in it a little bit," Mahomes said. "At the same time, I was No. 15 during my freshman year of basketball so I went back to that. I wanted to make my own number and do a new thing in this next chapter in life."

Popular Patrick

The limelight isn't too bright for one of the game's biggest superstars, and that's because he takes steps to stay out of it when he can. On the same day he was named AFC offensive player of the week for the second straight week to start the 2018 season, Mahomes spent his 23rd birthday at home.

"For my birthday, I came here and watched some film then I went home," he said. "I didn't want to go to dinner. My girlfriend had gotten me a cake so I just ordered Rye to go on Postmates.

"After I'm done with the day here, I don't like leaving the house so I usually just try to order something to go, and I have Fitstyle Foods that provides me meals. I usually eat that or to-go food."

Mahomes also admitted that he's a big fan of ketchup. He puts it on everything from macaroni and cheese to steaks. He later signed an endorsement

Kansas City hasn't been the same since Patrick Mahomes exploded onto the scene. (Scott Winters/Icon Sportswire)

deal with Hunt's ketchup and plans were in the works to launch a new cereal dubbed "Mahomes Magic Crunch."

Mahomes also launched his own official online merchandise store at Mahomes15.com. Fans can purchase T-shirts, hats, hoodies and other items as well as book Mahomes for speaking engagements, endorsements, personal appearances or corporate events.

Mahomes also is quite active on Twitter and Instagram. He has 400,000 followers on Twitter, a million followers on Instagram, and his popularity grows by the day.

"The people I've been around at Texas Tech and my hometown are great people," he said. "And then the people I'm here with now in Kansas City are great people. I've been lucky enough to be around a lot of people that care about me as much as a person as a player, so to have them reach out to me is always special."

When Mahomes does step out into the public eye, it's often at concerts or sporting events. One night in May 2018, he took in the NASCAR race at Kansas Speedway, rocking a sleeveless Kansas City T-Bones jersey with jean shorts, or "jorts," as the young people call them today.

Mahomes later was spotted at the Jason Aldean and Kenny Chesney concerts and threw out the first pitch at a Royals game. In November, he led the "I Believe" chant at Sporting KC's home playoff match against Portland.

A KC A-lister, he enjoys interacting with fans but admits that during the season he doesn't have a lot of free time and tries to stay focused on football.

"When you're in this league, you have to do something every single day," he said. "You have off days, but those days you're usually watching film so there's not really enough time to go out and do stuff and be out too late. So I try to focus in on being in the same routine every single day. I kind of do my certain things at the facility, I go home and do the same stuff there it seems like every single day and that does benefit me of not having to do anything extra.

"Alex did the same thing, he watched these games on this day and these games on this day and focused on this this day. And I've kind of taken stuff from that and made it my own so I'm prepared for every single situation."

Passing Lenny the Cool

In 1964, Len Dawson set a franchise single-season record with 30 touchdown passes. Back then teams played 14 games in the regular season. Fast forward to Week 10 in 2018 when Mahomes fired two TD passes against the Cardinals to break Dawson's single-season mark.

"I got to talk to Len about it and he was so far advanced in his time," Mahomes said. "For that record to stand this long… You throw 30 touchdowns in today's league, where there's a lot more passing, you're still having a great season. And so for him to be that advanced—and he won a Super Bowl here and he's one of the best quarterbacks to ever play—it is really an honor to be able to be close and even mentioned with his name in a single-season record like that."

When Dawson played, the AFL was considered a pass-happy league. Like Mahomes, Dawson had plenty of weapons but he never threw for 3,000 yards in a season. Mahomes eclipsed the 3,000-yard mark in Week 10.

Mahomes finished the season throwing for 5,097 yards and 50 touchdowns, his last coming on an 89-yard bomb to DeMarcus Robinson in Week 17 against the Raiders. Mahomes, at age 23, became just the second player in NFL history to throw for 5,000 yards and 50 touchdowns in a season.

"I'm not real big on numbers," Reid said. "But that was a pretty impressive deal, I will say."

MVPat

No "Air Raid" quarterback has had much success in the NFL—until Mahomes. In his first season as a starter, Mahomes made the Pro Bowl, won the NFL Offensive Player of the Year award and was named NFL MVP, becoming the first Chiefs player to win the award.

"I want to thank Chiefs Kingdom," Mahomes said with trophy in hand. "Your passion and love is unmatched. You're here, no matter when and where. This is just the beginning. We've got a long ways to go. Thank you!"

Mahomes' success didn't come easy. For starters, installing Reid's playbook is a lengthy process, and for Mahomes, one that entails putting pen to paper.

"It's a ton of writing down," Mahomes said. "I'll write the same play down three or four times until it sticks in my head. That's the biggest thing for me. I will use notecards and go through the formations and stuff like that. For the most part, it's a matter of writing it down a ton."

And after the install, there's still that whole matter of producing. For a while during training camp in 2018, Mahomes averaged about an interception per day and sometimes even called the wrong play in the huddle.

"From where he started to where he is at now has been tremendous," Reid said. "He's come quite a ways."

Mahomes admits he couldn't have done it without Reid, the same coach who helped guide Brett Favre and Donovan McNabb to Super Bowls when they were young players.

"Coach Reid, he's always going to push me," Mahomes said. "He's never going to be satisfied with what I'm doing, where I'm at. But that's how I feel about myself. You never want to be satisfied with one good performance, you want to make sure you can sustain that for a whole entire season or a whole entire career and I love that.

"And I think I said it in training camp, but I think he's always asking me questions in front of the team to make sure that I'm ready for every aspect and anything that could happen, and I like that because it challenges me to be the best I can every day."

Once upon a time, the words "best ever" and "Chiefs quarterback" appearing in the same sentence only happened in punchlines, or during the two seasons the Chiefs got to call Joe Montana their own. Now with Mahomes, those words are being thrown around by some of the greatest, including Favre, who once said Mahomes had the talent to be the best ever at the position. Only time will tell, but you can bet Mahomes will give it his best shot.

"That's awesome for him to say," Mahomes said of Favre. "That's someone I looked up to growing up and playing football. But there's still a long way to go for that. I'm just going to try to get better every day and hopefully we can have a lot of success."

CHAPTER 6
RUNNING BACKS

Mack Lee Hill

The history of Chiefs running backs is both great and tragic. Record-breaking runners have given fans countless wonderful memories but some have been taken far too soon.

Mack Lee Hill was one such player. Hill played just two seasons for the Chiefs (1964-65) but his presence is felt by the team even today as the Chiefs' Rookie of the Year award is named after him.

At 5-foot-11 and weighing 225 pounds, the muscular man they called "the Truck" made Kansas City's roster in 1964 as an undrafted free agent out of Southern University. The Chiefs were the only team to show interest in Hill and he signed for a meager $300, which was owed only if he made the team.

Hill had a solid rookie season and was the team's second-leading rusher, carrying 105 times for 567 yards and four touchdowns. His 5.5 yards per carry average led the league and he was selected to the Pro Bowl.

In his second year, Hill was even better. He rushed for 627 yards and a league-best 5.0 yards per attempt through the first 13 games. But that week at Buffalo, Hill tore a ligament in his right knee during the third quarter after catching a pass. Hill rushed eight times for 22 yards and caught four passes for 39 yards that day in the team's 34-25 defeat to Jack Kemp and the Bills.

On the plane ride home, Hill's knee began to swell up. Hill had a lifelong fear of doctors and hospitals and wanted desperately to avoid surgery, but team physician Dr. Joseph Lichtor said surgery was a must. So on Dec. 13, 1965, Hill checked into the Menorah Medical Center in Overland Park to get the knee fixed. The surgery went well but what happened afterward is still a bit of a mystery.

The following day, while getting ready to be transported to his room, doctors were putting a cast on Hill's knee when an anesthesiologist noticed the breathing machine Hill was on was unusually warm. Doctors took his temperature and the thermometer read 108 degrees. Hill then went into convulsions and doctors worked vigorously for two hours to cool him down, soaking his body in alcohol and surrounding him with ice. But nothing worked and he died later that afternoon. He was just 25.

The following month, it was determined that Hill died from "an acute heat stroke triggered by causes unproved." Pathologists also believed that Hill's muscular body might have actually worked against him, stating that in "heavily muscled persons a vicious cycle reaction may sometimes occur. The muscles create heat, which under anesthetic and surgical stress may incite oxygen lack and lead to a ventilation crisis."

At his eulogy, Len Dawson said Hill's memory would live on.

"Mack Lee Hill will never be forgotten in the hearts and minds of many of us, for Mack has set an example of living and competing for all of us to try to follow," Dawson said.

Hill's death marked the second time in three years the Chiefs had lost a player. In 1963, during the team's first season in Kansas City, the Chiefs played the Houston Oilers in an exhibition game in Wichita. Rookie running back Stone Johnson broke his neck while making a block on a kickoff return and died 10 days later.

Johnson ran the 200-meter dash for the U.S. in the 1960 Olympics in Rome but never played in a regular season game for the Chiefs. Still, the team retired Johnson's No. 33 as well as Hill's No. 36. Sadly, another Chiefs running back would lose his life decades later trying to lend a helping hand.

Joe Delaney

In life, we all need heroes. Whether it's a rough day at work, paying the bills or just getting through any of the other countless stresses that daily life can bring, sometimes when we need it the most a hero arrives. This hero can come in many different forms.

Joe Delaney was a real-life hero who died trying to save three boys from drowning in a pond in Monroe, La. Delaney did not know how to swim but jumped in anyway.

Delaney grew up in Haughton, a small town just east of Shreveport. He played football in high school and was a standout wide receiver. He also ran track and once ran the 100-yard dash in 9.4 seconds. At Northwestern State, a small college about an hour and a half south of Haughton, Delaney made the transition to running back even though he was only 5-foot-10 and weighed 185 pounds.

His blazing speed helped him get noticed by scouts, and the Chiefs picked him in the second round of the 1981 draft. At the time, the Chiefs were a struggling franchise and needed help at pretty much every position and Delaney infused a new energy to the team as his electrifying runs brought hope for the future. He also connected immediately with fans and teammates.

As a rookie, Delaney rushed for 1,121 yards and three touchdowns and caught 22 passes for 246 yards. He was named team MVP, won AFC Rookie of the Year and started in the Pro Bowl.

In the strike-shortened 1982 season, Delaney played in eight of the nine games but injuries slowed him down and he rushed for only 380 yards. That offseason, Delaney returned to his home state and on June 29, 1983, he and a few friends decided to attend a "Kids Day" festival in Monroe, about an hour's drive from Haughton.

On that hot summer afternoon, three young boys—11-year-old Harry Holland Jr., his 10-year-old brother LeMarkits and their 11-year old cousin Lancer Perkins—were playing and went too far out in a man-made pond that had been undergoing construction for a waterslide. Delaney heard their cries for help and ran in after them. The pit was 20 feet deep.

Water filled LeMarkits' lungs as he was being pulled to the bottom. Then a hand reached out and grabbed his shoulder, and Delaney heaved him out of the deep water.

Delaney soon dived in for the other two boys below the surface. People gathered along the bank and waited for him to come up, but he never did. He drowned along with Harry and Lancer. Delaney was just 24.

Buried on the Fourth of July, more than 3,000 people attended Delaney's funeral at his high school gym. President Ronald Reagan awarded him the Presidential Citizen Medal and a park was later named in his honor.

Since his death, no Chiefs player has worn his No. 37. Delaney was inducted into the College Football Hall of Fame in 1997 and the Chiefs Hall of Fame in 2004. Following Delaney's death, the "37 Forever Foundation" was formed, working to provide swimming lessons for kids.

Christian Okoye

From the moment he stepped onto the football field, Christian Okoye was a huge hit. But if you ever get the chance to talk to him, you'll quickly notice he's really a gentle giant.

At 6-foot-1 and 260 pounds, and wearing shoulder pads the size of boulders, Okoye was quite intimidating to defenders. He could also run over defensive tackles and linebackers and outrun defensive backs with ease.

Okoye played for the Chiefs from 1987 to 1992, retiring as the team's all-time leading rusher with 4,897 yards to go with 40 touchdowns. Though his career was short, he's easily one of the most popular Chiefs of all time. Okoye said one of the things he's most proud of is that he spent his entire career with the Chiefs.

"It means a lot," Okoye said with that warm, inviting smile. "I only played for the Chiefs. I didn't play for anybody else. Not too many people can say that. And coming back over here, it's like coming home.

"I love the fans here and the fans love me. So I truly, truly enjoy coming to Kansas City because of the people. The Hunt family, the coaches, players and just the passion that you see on the field during the game from the fans, it's incredible."

The Nigerian Nightmare

Okoye was born in Enugu, Nigeria, on Aug. 16, 1961. He grew up during the Nigerian Civil War where he and his family saw terrible things. Okoye found solace playing soccer and throwing the shotput and discus in track.

Kansas City Chiefs running back Christian Okoye (35) runs through the tackle of Detroit's Herb Welch on Oct. 14, 1990, at Arrowhead Stadium. Okoye ran for 91 yards and two scores that day in the Chiefs' 43-24 win. (Kevin Reece/Icon Sportswire)

His coach, Patrick Anukwa, had connections in the United States, and Okoye became friends with Nigerian sprinter Innocent Egbunike, who had just competed in the 1980 Olympics in Moscow. Okoye's mother had died a couple years before and Egbunike's mother took him in and raised him as her own.

Egbunike wanted to go to America and attend a school in southern California so he could train for the 1984 Olympics in Los Angeles. USC was among several schools interested in Egbunike, but his mother wanted him to go to a Christian school. She also wanted him to help Okoye out if an opportunity presented itself and it did.

Egbunike chose Azusa Pacific—a tiny NAIA school about 30 minutes east of L.A. He told track coach Terry Franson about Okoye and an offer was made. Okoye went to the U.S. in 1982 and competed in the hammer throw, discus and shotput. He won seven national titles along the way and became one of the best throwers in the world.

Determined to be on the Nigerian Olympic team, Okoye once appeared to be a lock. But Nigeria ultimately left him off the roster. Okoye was devastated but went to the Games and watched Egbunike win a bronze medal in the 1,600 relay at the same time the discus competition was being held.

Okoye was a top-five thrower in the nation with a personal-best of 64.87 meters and likely could have medaled at the Games had he not been left off the team. Okoye could have tried to be on the 1988 Olympic team, but he was so disappointed—and believed his home country might omit him again—he decided to finish school and try something else at age 23.

That something else was football.

Okoye had no experience playing the game. But when he saw a highlight reel of Super Bowl XVIII between the Raiders and Redskins on the news one night, one play stood out. It was a run by the Raiders' Marcus Allen where he started left, spun back around, found a hole up the middle and veered down the sideline for a 74-yard touchdown.

Mesmerized by this, Okoye went to Azusa Pacific football coach Jim Milhon and asked him what position Allen played.

"Running back," Milhon said.

"I want to play that," Okoye said.

Unsure of what he had in a football player, Milhon had Okoye run the 40-yard dash. After Okoye crossed the line, Milhon looked at his watch. It read 4.38.

In three seasons at Azusa Pacific, Okoye rushed for 3,500 yards, scored 34 touchdowns and averaged nearly 7 yards per carry. Okoye, however, was left off all the senior all-star game rosters until Heisman runner-up Paul Palmer elected not to play in the Senior Bowl.

Okoye took the Temple standout's spot and scored four touchdowns. NFL scouts were blown away by Okoye's combination of power and speed. He had a 34-inch waist, 28-inch thighs and a vertical leap of 35 inches. He also bench pressed 400 pounds and could squat 725 pounds.

After selecting Palmer in the first round of the 1987 draft, the Chiefs picked the 25-year-old Okoye in the second round. The Chiefs originally tried him out at fullback, but Okoye's inexperience with blocking quickly showed. However, when he ran the ball, he couldn't be stopped.

Not long after he was drafted, Chiefs quarterback Bill Kenney invited Okoye to his farm for dinner. Kenney's kids each had a pet goat and Okoye asked Kenney if he could have one—to eat! Growing up, goat was one of Okoye's favorite meals back in Nigeria.

Though Kenney said no, Okoye eventually found a taker, paying $25 for a goat and another $25 to have it slaughtered.

In his NFL debut against the San Diego Chargers in Week 1, Okoye rushed 21 times for 105 yards and a touchdown in the Chiefs' 20-13 win. In the huddle after one play, starting tackle Irv Eatman called Okoye the "Nigerian Nightmare" and the nickname stuck.

More than a game

Okoye was a perfect fit in Marty Schottenheimer's smash-mouth offense. In 1989, he rushed for an NFL-best 1,480 yards on a whopping 370 carries, which also led the league. Okoye made the Pro Bowl in 1989 and 1991, the same year Nintendo released Tecmo Super Bowl.

Okoye was one of the best players on the game with his speed and power. Ironically, he never played it during his playing career.

"I heard about that," Okoye said. "I didn't play it until somebody did a story on it just a few years ago. It was NFL Films that did a story on it and they brought me the game and actually made me play so they could film it. And then (in 2016) the Chiefs did a little blurb on it and had me sit in the stands and they played it on the jumbotron. So it was nice."

But at the height of his career, Okoye went through a real nightmare. Shortly before training camp in 1990, he and his then-wife had a child that died about 30 minutes after it was born. Still grieving, he reported late to training camp.

Uncertain how long Okoye would be away from the team, the Chiefs needed another big back and signed free agent Barry Word. That season both running backs carried the ball more than 200 times and combined for 1,800 yards on the ground.

But injuries and years of hard running took a toll on Okoye and he retired after the 1992 season at age 31. Had he played another year, Okoye said he might not be able to walk so he had to step away.

Though his career was short, Okoye has definitely had an impact across the globe. In 1990, he started the Christian Okoye Foundation, which works with at-risk youth. His foundation also has free sports camps during the summer, and Okoye said he returns to his home country whenever he can, proving his heart is just as big as he is.

"I try to go back once or twice a year now because I just set up a children's youth program in Nigeria and it happens every week," Okoye said. "We work with kids out there on education and sports so I'm able to go back now and kind of see how it's going."

For all his travels, though, there's no place like Kansas City.

"Coming back to Arrowhead Stadium is always a treat," Okoye said. "This is where I made my living. It brings back memories, especially on alumni weekend. It's a time that you get together with your old teammates and former players, even people that you didn't play with.

"It brings everybody together. We have a good time reminiscing, talking to each other and spending time with each other."

Marcus Allen

On March 1, 1993, Marcus Allen officially regained his freedom. For six long years he feuded with Raiders owner Al Davis, and he spent the last four of those standing on the sideline watching Bo Jackson, Roger Craig, Eric Dickerson and others play in front of him. But when the NFL granted unrestricted free agency, Allen was free to sign elsewhere.

Allen essentially created his own escape route in 1991 by joining with other active players in an antitrust lawsuit against the NFL. Ironically, on the day the Raiders found out Allen joined the lawsuit he was demoted to third-string and took the field only on third down or short-yardage situations.

Allen spent the first 11 years of his career with the Raiders and was MVP of Super Bowl XVIII, but a running back entering the free-agent field at age 33 was cause for concern for some within the Chiefs organization. Coach Marty Schottenheimer felt otherwise. From having watched Allen on tape and seeing him play firsthand for years, Schottenheimer believed Allen's inactivity would only extend his career.

Schottenheimer called Allen once a week for several months, trying to reel him in by convincing him that he would be a great fit in his new West Coast offense—as the backup running back to Harvey Williams and as a backup fullback—a position he also played while being in Davis' doghouse.

"Marty was persistent," Allen said back then. "He said, 'We want you. We want you to be part of this team and part of this organization.' That's what I wanted to hear."

The Packers, Seahawks and Falcons were interested in Allen, but the thought of playing two times a year against the Raiders made Allen smile. And on June 9, 1993, Allen and the Chiefs agreed to a three-year deal.

"The last couple of years I haven't had much enthusiasm and it showed in my play," Allen said. "Believe me, there's a lot left."

The signing of Allen completed a makeover for the Chiefs offense. Two months earlier, the Chiefs swung a deal for Joe Montana—another veteran looking for a new team and an opportunity to keep playing.

Allen took his time picking his new surroundings, but it wasn't until the Chiefs completed the trade for Montana that he started to see himself in red and gold.

"You'd have to be crazy not to take advantage of an opportunity to play with Joe Montana," Allen said. "I want to go to the Super Bowl, and Kansas City does, too. Hopefully I can help them get there."

Initially, Allen didn't start in 1993, but his impact was immediately felt on the field and in the locker room. In the season opener at Tampa Bay, he carried 13 times for 79 yards and caught the last of three touchdown passes from Montana in the Chiefs' 27-3 win.

By midseason, Allen became the team's starting tailback and finished the year with 764 yards and 12 touchdowns to go with 34 catches for 238 yards and three scores. Known for his patience, Allen had a knack for crossing the goal line and converting on third down. He helped lead the Chiefs to an 11-5 record and the AFC West title. He was named team MVP, NFL Comeback Player of the Year and made the Pro Bowl for the first time in six years.

Allen also proved tough to stop in the playoffs, rushing for 67 yards and a touchdown against the Steelers and rushing for 74 yards and a game-clinching touchdown against the Oilers in the divisional round.

Against the Bills in the AFC championship game, Allen rushed 18 times for 50 yards and a touchdown, but the Chiefs were blown out 30-13. In October 1995, Allen scored the 100th rushing touchdown of his career, flying over the goal line on a snowy day at Denver. On Thanksgiving Day in 1996, he scored on a pair of 1-yard runs at Detroit to break Walter Payton's career rushing touchdown record with 112.

Though Allen didn't put on a Chiefs uniform until he was deep into his 30s, the Chiefs went 9-1 in his 10 career games against the Raiders. Allen retired following the 1997 season, ending his Chiefs' career with 3,698 yards rushing and a then-team record 44 touchdowns to go with 141 receptions for 1,153 yards—also the most by a Chiefs running back at the time.

Allen had one year remaining on his contract, but at age 37 it was time to step away.

"The records, I'm proud of," Allen said. "But it's the people I've worked with on a day-to-day basis who realty made the game for me.

"The most important thing has always been the journey, and the people you meet and gain respect for in the common struggle to achieve something."

Priest Holmes

By the looks of it, Priest Holmes could still play. But football can be a cruel sport, and Holmes knows that firsthand.

During the Chiefs annual alumni weekend in October 2017 at Arrowhead Stadium, Holmes mingled with former teammates and fellow Chiefs greats. Still looking fit and youthful, Holmes smiled as he recalled his glory days in Chiefs red and gold.

"I can't walk through this stadium without feeling it," Holmes said. "Outside of the aesthetics that look so much better now, but it definitely is a great place. It was my home for seven years, and I just recently moved in 2014. So although I've moved, and I'm primarily in San Antonio, this is still my second home."

Kansas City Chiefs running back Priest Holmes (31) runs through a gaping hole courtesy of Pro Football Hall of Fame lineman Will Shields (68) during a game against the Washington Redskins on Oct. 16, 2005, at Arrowhead Stadium. (Denny Medley/Icon Sportswire)

Holmes was signed by the Chiefs as a free agent in 2001, having spent his first four seasons with Baltimore. Holmes' signing with the Chiefs didn't come with much fanfare. But before his career was over he was loved by everyone in Kansas City.

Known for being quiet and humble, Holmes was originally signed as an undrafted free agent in 1997 with the Ravens. Though he won a Super Bowl with Baltimore in 2000, he was primarily a backup, just like when he played in college at the University of Texas.

Holmes played for the Longhorns from 1992-96, missing the 1995 season with an ACL injury. When he arrived on campus in 1992, he was known as Anthony Holmes, but "Priest" would soon become a household name. In the 1994 Sun Bowl, Holmes rushed for 161 yards and four touchdowns against Mack Brown's North Carolina Tar Heels.

Brown, of course, went on to coach at Texas from 1998-2013, inheriting one of the best running backs in college football history in Ricky Williams. Williams played at Texas from 1995-98. During his sophomore season, he began the year as the lead blocker for Holmes, who was a fifth-year senior.

That arrangement didn't last as Holmes had injury problems and missed two games that year while Williams was well on his way to a record-breaking career. While at UT, Williams looked up to Holmes. And though Holmes was relegated to backup duty, he capped his senior season in style.

In the inaugural Big 12 championship game against Nebraska, Holmes ran nine times for 130 yards and scored three touchdowns, leading the Longhorns to a 37-27 win over the heavily favored Huskers to capture the first Big 12 title. Dick Vermeil, who would later become his coach in Kansas City, broadcast that game before he played a key role along with former general manager Carl Peterson and quarterback Trent Green in bringing Holmes to Kansas City.

"They were instrumental, and I guess the person that would be the biggest piece of me coming here with the Chiefs was Trent Green," Holmes said.

"Because if Coach Vermeil went with Trent Green, he was going to go with a running back that had some time in the league, and I had been in Baltimore for four years.

"Had they not went with Trent, they would have elected to go with a younger quarterback and a younger running back. So I'm excited that went through and it allowed me the opportunity to be here and we made some magic when we were here."

At 5-foot-9 and 213 pounds, Holmes didn't have blazing speed but made up for it in other ways. His vision and patience as a runner, combined with his stout nature, made him tough to tackle, and he ran hard and with power.

In his first season with the Chiefs, Holmes rushed for 1,555 yards and eight touchdowns. He also caught 62 passes, showing his dual-threat capability on the way to his first of three straight Pro Bowls.

In 2002, he rushed for 1,615 yards and 21 touchdowns, often flying over the top of the pile at the goal line. In 2003, Holmes rushed for 1,420 yards and scored 27 touchdowns on the ground, setting a then-NFL record for rushing touchdowns in a season.

While Holmes enjoyed another outstanding year, the Chiefs went 13-3 and won the division for the first time since 1997. But the Chiefs lost at home to Peyton Manning and the Colts in a shootout 38-31 in the divisional round of the playoffs in a game that had no punts.

Holmes ran wild that afternoon, rushing 24 times for 176 yards and two scores. While the 1997 team's playoff loss to Denver is still tough to take for Chiefs fans more than 20 years later, Holmes can relate. The playoff loss to the Colts in January 2004 still gnaws at him.

"That one's mine," he said.

After that playoff performance, Holmes' career began to go south because of injuries. In 2004, his season was cut short after eight games because of lingering effects from a helmet-to-helmet hit. In October 2005, Holmes was placed on injured reserve after injuring his neck and spine in a game against the San Diego Chargers.

Holmes was forced to sit out the 2006 season, but before training camp opened in 2007, he had a dream and saw himself playing again. So he called the Chiefs and said he wanted to make a comeback. Holmes returned to the field in Week 7 that year against the Raiders but his comeback was short.

He played in just four games as another neck injury made him opt for retirement. Holmes retired as the team's all-time leader in several categories including, career rushing yards (6,070), rushing touchdowns (76) and total touchdowns (83).

Since his playing days ended, Holmes has remained active in the community. Back home in Texas, he provides scholarships for San Antonio Bexar County students and still finds a way to give back to the Chiefs as an advocate for former players.

"Those are two things that are very near and dear to my heart, making sure I provide the resources for former players and also providing scholarships for Bexar County graduating seniors," Holmes said.

Though Holmes lives in Texas, he still makes it to Kansas City as often as he can, and that's important to both him and the Chiefs.

"I try to get back for at least two games each year," Holmes said. "One of them always includes the alumni weekend and then also during the spring, generally right around draft time. I was able to go talk to the rookies and kind of meet them at my level and then give them some perspective on where they're at in introducing this new career that they're going to have."

Jamaal Charles

Chiefs-Broncos games are never just another game. And for Jamaal Charles, the matchup on Oct. 30, 2017, at Arrowhead Stadium had a little more meaning.

On that night, Charles wore orange, white and blue and was a backup running back for the Broncos. From 2008-16, Charles was the Chiefs' best player, slicing his way to becoming the team's all-time leading rusher with 7,260 yards before knee injuries slowed him down and the team released him in a cost-cutting move before the 2017 season.

Charles eventually signed a one-year deal with the Broncos. As a kid, Charles was a big John Elway fan, and the Broncos naturally were his favorite team. So when they came calling it made perfect sense for Charles to sign with the Chiefs' AFC West rival.

In his return to Arrowhead Stadium, Charles rushed eight times for 39 yards. When he took the field for the first time as a visitor, he couldn't help but feel a bit out of place.

"It felt weird," Charles said after the game.

As surreal as it was for Charles, there was one Chiefs' tradition that continued even though he was a member of the Broncos. Prior to the game, Charles and some of his former Chiefs teammates got together and started to jump around and hoot and holler.

"We were excited," Charles said. "We jumped around. I used to always jump around so it started bringing back memories and we just talked. It was good seeing everybody who I worked hard with when I was here."

Charles' return to Kansas City didn't go quite as he had hoped. Though an 18-yard burst showed some of the speed he once had was still there, he also had a fumble, and the Broncos lost 29-19. On the fumble, Charles was fighting for more yards—a mistake he later admitted to.

"I was trying to do too much," Charles said. "I was excited to be here. I wanted to make plays. I wanted to show everyone I could still play and I think I just did too much trying to continue to move my leg. I should have just gave myself up.

"I was trying to get some more yards, some extra yards, and I was just doing too much, and that was on me. I was the captain tonight. I felt like I didn't perform up to a captain's standards. I just got to go back and work on my craft."

Running down a dream

With the Chiefs, there was little Charles needed to work on. Already blessed with world-class speed, his agility and ability to cut back across the grain, spin and weave all over the field made him an instant fan favorite.

"It's funny, it was almost like practice," Chiefs linebacker Justin Houston said of facing Charles for the first time. "But you know in practice we couldn't hit him. So it felt good hitting him. I told him my first time hitting him felt good. He's still got his wheels."

Ironically, Charles' career took off after he was inserted into the starting lineup when the team parted ways with Larry Johnson, whose career was plagued by problems off the field. The Chiefs drafted Johnson, a bruiser out of Penn State, in the first round of the 2003 draft and he was just 75 yards away from passing Priest Holmes as the team's all-time leading rusher when the Chiefs finally cut the cord with him in November 2009.

At one point, fans were so adamant that Johnson not be given the opportunity to surpass Holmes in the record books, they started an online petition begging the Chiefs to deactivate him. The petition had more than 32,000 signatures, and the team noticed. Johnson was inactive for two games and suspended for another before his release.

Chiefs running back Jamaal Charles (25) breaks loose for a 39-yard touchdown run in the second half against the Buffalo Bills on Nov. 9, 2014, at Ralph Wilson Stadium. Charles played nine seasons with the Chiefs and is the team's all-time leading rusher with 7,260 yards. (Kellen Micah/Icon Sportswire)

With Johnson out and Charles in, the ground game picked up steam. Charles went on to rush for 1,120 yards and seven touchdowns while leading the league with a 5.9 yard average in 2009. He capped off the year with a 259-yard performance at Denver in the last game of the season.

Charles rushed for 1,467 yards in 2010 and made the first of four Pro Bowls. In 2011, he tore his left ACL against the Lions in Week 2 and missed the rest of the season. In 2012, Charles came back and rushed for a career-best 1,509 yards, the lone highlight in a dreadful and even deadly 2-14 season for the Chiefs.

On the first day of December, starting linebacker Jovan Belcher fatally shot his girlfriend, Kassandra Perkins, at the couple's home in Kansas City. Belcher then drove to Arrowhead Stadium and shot himself in the parking lot in front of team executives.

Perkins was a first cousin to Charles' wife, Whitney. Charles actually introduced Belcher and Perkins in 2010. The couple also had a newborn baby at the time of the shooting. The Chiefs were scheduled to play the Panthers the next day at Arrowhead Stadium and for a while it looked like the game might be canceled. But the Chiefs opted to play, and Charles rushed for 127 yards in a 27-21 win.

In 2013, with Andy Reid at the helm, Charles enjoyed his best season. He rushed for 1,287 yards and 12 touchdowns and caught 70 passes for 693 yards and seven touchdowns.

Charles again stayed healthy in 2014, rushing for 1,033 yards. But in the fifth game of the 2015 season, he tore his right ACL, and at age 29 Charles underwent his second major knee surgery.

Charles took longer to recover, and the team held him out of the first three games in 2016. But Charles only played in three more games—carrying the ball a grand total of 12 times for 40 yards—as his knees couldn't hold up. The Chiefs placed him on injured reserve, and he underwent a third surgery on his knees.

At least two NFL teams told Charles to retire prior to the 2017 season. Charles, however, refused to give in.

"I'm pulling for him," Chiefs coach Andy Reid said then. "He's that kind of person. He'll go down as one of the all-time greats, not only with the Chiefs, but also the NFL."

Though Canton might be a destination, Charles, who signed a one-day contract with the Chiefs in May 2019 and officially retired, will someday be in the Chiefs' Hall of Fame. Not bad for a third-round pick who grew up in Port Arthur, Texas, before becoming a football and track star at Texas with the Longhorns

Learning to fly

As a kid, Charles had a learning disability. He had trouble reading and speaking and was teased a lot.

As a third-grader, Charles was inserted into special-education classes. Turns out he had trouble understanding grammar, specifically commas and periods, which made his sentences a convoluted mess.

While the rest of the kids in school got to go on field trips to Six Flags and other fun places, at age 10 Charles and his classmates went to the 1996 Special Olympics in nearby Beaumont where he won the 100-meter dash, 200 hurdles and the long jump.

There Charles gained a newfound confidence that he could overcome his learning disability and somehow flourish despite being raised in Port Arthur, Texas, a town known for its oil refineries and crime. In his teens, Charles still had anxiety about reading and school, but with the help of his teachers, he improved.

As a freshman at Texas, he rushed for 878 yards and averaged 7.8 yards per attempt, helping lead the Longhorns to the national title. A few months later,

Charles won the Big 12 Outdoor in the 100-meter dash with a time of 10.23 seconds. As a sophomore, he earned second-team academic All-Big 12 honors and often sat in the front of the classroom, whereas in his younger days he would sit in the back of the room afraid to raise his hand.

During the opening ceremonies for the 2015 Special Olympics World Games in Los Angeles, Charles led the athletes' oath in a touching, heartfelt speech.

"I was afraid, I was lost," Charles told the crowd. "People made fun of me. They said I would never go anywhere. But I learned I can fly. The Special Olympics gave me the chance to discover the talent I did not know I had.

"When I competed in the Special Olympics, I found out just how fast I was. I stood high on the podium, getting the gold medal in track and field. And when I found out how fast I was, I was blessed with a new confidence. The confidence turned into courage, the courage to be the best that I can every day."

In 2016, Charles published a children's book, *The Middle School Rules of Jamaal Charles*, documenting his struggles as a child and rise to NFL star. Though Charles did not spend his entire career with the Chiefs, he'll always be remembered for what he did in red and gold. Even on a night he wore white and blue in a stadium filled with red.

"Yeah, it was pretty cool, you know what I'm saying?" Charles said. "People were missing me and just talking about 'welcome back' and everything. They were giving me good compliments."

CHAPTER 7
FULLBACK

Tony Richardson

Fullbacks are a dying breed in the NFL, but for 10 years Tony Richardson was an integral part of the Chiefs offense as a blocking back.

Richardson played for the Chiefs from 1995-2005 and made the Pro Bowl twice. During his first season in Kansas City, he played on special teams and became a valuable asset as Marcus Allen's lead blocker in goal-line and short-yardage situations. In later years, he cleared paths for Priest Holmes and Larry Johnson as they led the NFL in rushing in 2001 and 2005, respectively.

"I always kind of considered myself an extension of the offensive line," Richardson said during his September 2016 induction into the Chiefs Hall of Fame.

An undrafted free agent out of Auburn, Richardson was on the Dallas Cowboys practice squad for a year before signing with the Chiefs. His role with club eventually increased and he became a starter in 1999.

Richardson finished his career playing two seasons with the Vikings and three with the Jets and retired following the 2010 season. When he returned to Kansas City for his induction, seeing his name on the Ring of Honor was overwhelming.

"It it's very humbling," Richardson said. "Coming into the league as an undrafted free agent and leaving the Dallas Cowboys practice squad, the number of times I ran out of that tunnel and saw Len Dawson, to see Jan Stenerud, Derrick Thomas."

"To see all those names, the guys that I played with, and obviously, some guys that I looked up to. To have my name up there with Christian Okoye—the list goes on and on. It just doesn't even seem real."

In addition to being one of the game's best blockers, Richardson was a versatile back. In 2000, he led the team in rushing with 697 yards. In his Chiefs career, he rushed for 1,576 yards and 15 touchdowns and caught 177 passes for 1,298 yards and seven touchdowns.

Leaving Kansas City was a difficult adjustment for Richardson, but now he'll always be a Chief.

"It was hard because Kansas City was home, it's family," he said." I would consider the Hunt family as part of my family. Obviously that's part of the business, unfortunately. Sometimes contracts don't get worked out, situations don't get worked out. But at the end of the day, now I'll be a part of Kansas City Chiefs history for the rest of my life."

CHAPTER 8
WIDE RECEIVERS

Otis Taylor

Throw the ball up, he'd get it. Need a down-field block? He'd make it. Tight-rope the sideline for a touchdown in the Super Bowl, he'd do it.

Otis Taylor could do most anything for the Chiefs—leap like a gazelle, catch anything remotely close to him, weave around defenders and run a sub-4.5 in the 40-yard dash. For 11 seasons (1965-75), Taylor was Len Dawson's favorite target, catching 410 passes for 7,306 yards (17.8 avg.) and 57 touchdowns. And at 6-foot-3 and 215 pounds, with his size and quickness, Taylor was in a class by himself.

Taylor was as physical a receiver as anyone in the league. And in Super Bowl IV against the Vikings, he used his speed and toughness to seal the Chiefs' win.

With the Chiefs leading 16-7 late in the third quarter, Dawson dropped back to pass and found Taylor on the right sideline. Taylor caught the ball and immediately spun out of Earsell Mackbee's tackle and scampered down the sideline. At the 15, he juked and stiff-armed Karl Kassukle before high-stepping into the end zone for a 46-yard touchdown in what would become the second-most memorable play in Chiefs history.

In the final game of the AFL, Taylor caught six passes for 81 yards and scored the memorable touchdown.

"I knew we needed to score because I remember the way Minnesota came back on the Rams," Taylor said after the game. "I got hit but spun away from

Kansas City wide receiver Otis Taylor (89) caught 410 passes for 7,306 yards and 57 touchdowns in 11 seasons with the Chiefs. (Kenneth Spencer Research Library, University of Kansas Libraries)

the first guy then I hit the last guy with my hand. I always try to punish a defender, just like they try to punish me."

Taylor's rise from underprivileged kid to NFL stardom is unique in many ways, but his story begins with him sneaking out the window of his hotel room.

The Babysitting Incident

In the 1960s, the AFL and NFL routinely battled over players in the draft. Each league could select a player in its draft, but with competition between the two leagues so fierce, getting them signed and delivered was more like something out of a James Bond movie.

In those days the NFL could "babysit" college players in an effort to keep them from talking with AFL teams. These babysitters often moved prospects around from motel to motel in an effort to keep their whereabouts under wraps so an AFL scout couldn't sneak in and sign them away at the last minute.

On the Friday after Thanksgiving in 1964, which was the day before both the AFL and NFL Draft, the Dallas Cowboys were babysitting Taylor, the standout wide receiver from Prairie View A&M, and his teammate and friend Seth Cartwright.

The Chiefs had a connection to Taylor in part-time scout Lloyd Wells, but he was in Nashville when he got a call from Lamar Hunt's secretary informing him that Taylor was on his way to Dallas with NFL babysitters for a pre-draft party.

Wells boarded the next plane bound for Dallas. Once there, he tried to track down where Taylor was staying. After calls to Taylor's mother and girlfriend, Wells eventually learned that he was staying at the Continental Inn in nearby Richardson, Texas.

Wells gave Chiefs GM Don Klosterman updates when he could, and he told Wells to tell Taylor that the red Thunderbird he wanted would be waiting for him when he got to Kansas City. Wells was a newspaper reporter and photographer in Taylor's hometown of Houston so the two had known each other for years. But to get past all the NFL handlers and guards without being noticed, Wells went undercover, strapping a camera across his neck and posing as a reporter who was on assignment to interview Taylor.

Inside Taylor's room, Wells convinced him to leave and sign with the Chiefs.

"Let's get out of here," Wells said.

"They're watching me," Taylor replied.

So Taylor insisted on leaving later that night. At about 3 a.m. Taylor called Wells to come pick him up and 30 minutes later Taylor snuck out the window and left in Wells' car. Earlier that day, a Cowboys agent spotted Wells and told him if he came back he would be arrested for trespassing. So fearing the Dallas airport might be staked out, Wells instead drove to Fort Worth, and he and

Taylor arrived in Kansas City a few hours later. By the end of the day, the Chiefs had drafted Taylor in the fourth round and signed him to a three-year contract worth $45,000.

Taylor then joined the Chiefs on their trip to New York to play the Jets. When they got back, he drove the T-Bird back home to Houston.

"The intrigue was marvelous," Hunt recalled in his autobiography *Lamar Hunt: A Life in Sports*. "The public loved it. I loved it."

The Ben Davidson Incident

The Chiefs-Raiders rivalry has always been pretty fierce, but on Nov. 1, 1970, it got violent. And Taylor was in the middle of it. The Chiefs were leading 17-14 with 1:08 to play in the fourth quarter when Dawson ran 19 yards for a game-clinching first down. After Dawson went down, he was speared by Raiders defensive end Ben Davidson.

Taylor immediately retaliated, punching Davidson and throwing him to the ground. Both benches cleared and a brawl ensued. Several minutes later after order was restored, personal-foul penalties were called on both teams.

Taylor was ejected, and the down had to be replayed. This time the Chiefs didn't convert on third down and had to punt. Oakland drove down the field, George Blanda kicked a field goal and the game ended in a tie.

After the game, Taylor told the Associated Press that he didn't understand why he was thrown out.

"I just grabbed Davidson and was holding him down," Taylor said. "He piled on Len with a pretty hard blow, and when Oakland takes a shot at him like that it's up to us to protect him."

Chiefs coach Hank Stram was trying to protect his two stars, but even he was at a loss for words after talking to the official.

"He didn't explain anything," Stram said at the time. "No one seems to know what happened."

Waiting game

The NFL Hall of Fame is dotted with players who have better statistics than Taylor, and likewise there are some who don't. But if you judge players based on impacting the game in their era, it's hard to find one who did so more than Taylor.

Taylor has waited nearly 40 years for the call to Canton, but he's never been a finalist despite being a three-time Pro Bowler and a first-team All-Pro.

"The guy I feel bad about is Otis," said Rick Gosselin, who made the Hall of Fame presentations for Buck Buchanan, Emmitt Thomas, Johnny Robinson and others. "I don't know what happened."

A spot in Canton, however, doesn't seem quite as important now as the effects of Parkinson's and dementia have left Taylor bedridden and on a feeding tube for more than a decade. Taylor, though, is still remembered as one of the all-time great Chiefs, something Stram saw coming when the young flanker was in just his second season as a pro.

"You have to see Taylor every day to realize how great he is," Stram said. "He's 6-3, weighs 215, has terrific speed and moves. He's also a very, very tough guy. He'll hit people and he's convinced he's the best."

Tyreek Hill

Wide receiver hasn't always been a position of strength for the Chiefs, but Tyreek Hill was quickly changing that until he was stopped in his tracks at least temporarily.

Hill, who might be the fastest player in the NFL and is probably the Chiefs' most talented receiver since Otis Taylor, set the club record for receiving yards in a season with 1,479 in 2018. He also had 87 catches and 12 touchdowns, earning his third straight Pro Bowl. But for as great as he's been on the field—Hill is already 11th all-time in team receiving yards (3,255) and touchdowns (25)—the Cheetah's future with the team is still somewhat in limbo at deadline for this book.

Kansas City wide receiver Tyreek Hill set the team record for receiving yards in a season with 1,479 in 2018. Here he is catching a touchdown pass against the Los Angeles Rams on Nov. 19, 2018. (Jordon Kelly/Icon Sportswire)

Hill was suspended by the club in April 2019 after KCTV-5 aired an audio recording in which his then-fiancée Crystal Espinal accused him of abusing their 3-year-old son. The recording was broadcast the same night as the first round of the NFL Draft and one day after Johnson County prosecutors said the criminal investigation involving Hill and Espinal was closed and no charges would be filed.

In the audio recording, Espinal tells Hill that when their son was asked about an injury to his arm, he said, "Daddy did it." Hill, however, denied any wrongdoing, saying, "He says Daddy does a lot of things." Espinal also said the child "is terrified of you." Hill replied, "You should be terrified of me, too, bitch."

A couple days later, Chiefs chairman Clark Hunt said he was "deeply disturbed" by the audio and didn't anticipate a quick resolution to cutting Hill or keeping him on the roster.

"He's not with the organization at this point, and we would expect that will be the case until we have a chance to work our way through whatever information we are able to get," Hunt said during the draft.

The Chiefs originally selected Hill in the fifth round—165th overall—in the 2016 draft. His selection caused an immediate outcry by fans and some media members as he arrived with a checkered past.

In December 2014, Hill was kicked off Oklahoma State's football team after he hit and choked Espinal, his then-pregnant girlfriend. Hill pled guilty to assault and got three years' probation. He began court-ordered counseling and eventually wound up playing his senior year at Division-II West Alabama. There he caught the attention of scouts and ran a blazing 4.25 on his pro day.

But some teams removed him from their draft boards entirely because of the assault charge at OSU. The Chiefs, however, saw a potential win-win in Hill. Prior to selecting him, the Chiefs did extensive research on his background, talking to former teammates and coaches and even the prosecutor of his case.

Hill hasn't said much about the incident since he was drafted, but he was remorseful and accepted responsibility.

"I don't blame nobody but myself," Hill said his rookie year. "It's my fault, it's my mistake."

Chiefs coach Andy Reid has been pretty generous when it comes to second chances, and at the time he believed Hill deserved one.

"Listen, I understand the situation," Reid said after the team drafted Hill. "I've seen different situations and I'm not here to judge. I am not the all-mighty. I'm not saying that at all by any means, but from what we gathered, and we tried to be as thorough as we could with it, we felt that he deserved an opportunity."

Hill quickly made the most of the opportunity, becoming both a top wideout and returner. Back in 1965, Bears rookie Gale Sayers, also known as the Kansas Comet, scored a touchdown rushing, receiving and on a kick return in a game against the Vikings. That feat stood for 51 years until November 2016 when Hill had a trifecta of his own, scoring on an 86-yard kick return, a 3-yard run and 3-yard reception in a win at Denver.

Hill returned two punts for scores as a rookie and has four punt return touchdowns in his career.

"Anytime he touches the ball, he is dynamic and he can score anytime," Chiefs special teams coach Dave Toub said. "If the punter makes a mistake, or gets a line-drive kick, or a kick that does not have a lot of hang time, or miss hits one, you know we have a chance."

In 2018 against the Cardinals, Hill, whose touchdown celebrations always include "the deuces," also showed he can make highlights in the stands. After scoring his second touchdown of the game he jumped into the crowd and took over the TV camera in the back of the end zone and filmed his teammates' celebration to his own touchdown.

"You all saw me up there, man?" Hill joked after the game. "I got some good camera skills. I did my thing. I'm just showing love to my teammates because I feel my teammates deserve it all. The offensive line deserves it, everybody."

That includes defensive lineman Chris Jones, who admired Hill's camera work even though it drew a penalty.

"That celebration was amazing," Jones said. "I know Coach Reid didn't like it. Coach Reid doesn't like celebrations that get penalties. I knew it was a good celebration, but I couldn't say too much about it because Coach Reid, his mustache started flaring up so I just try to keep it at a minimum."

With Hill the Chiefs have a game-changer. And throw in Patrick Mahomes at quarterback, they easily have the best down-field passing combination in the NFL.

"I feel like me and Pat could be the best," Hill once said.

Without Hill, the Chiefs offense looks quite a bit different. Whether Hill gets another opportunity with the Chiefs remains to be seen but he was still on the roster. A suspension by the NFL, a trade, or a release from the Chiefs are all possibilities for Hill. And depending on what else comes to light, so is keeping him on the team and playing him. But Hunt said the Chiefs will make the right call.

"Tyreek's not with the franchise right now," Hunt said. "And we're going to go through the process, and as Brett (Veach) said on Thursday (draft) night, we'll make the right decision about Tyreek at the right time."

CHAPTER 9
TIGHT ENDS

Tony Gonzalez

On Dec. 13, 2018, 21 years after the Chiefs drafted him with the 13th pick in the NFL Draft, Tony Gonzalez became the 44th player inducted into the Chiefs' Ring of Honor.

Canton, Ohio, is the next stop for Gonzalez, the greatest tight end to ever play the game. He'll reach that destination in August 2019, but his return to Kansas City on that mid-December night is something he'll never forget.

"It's the pinnacle of everything that I've done because I know sports is over," Gonzalez said. "And I don't even want to play anymore. People ask me, 'Do you want to get out there and play?' Maybe for a quick second when I was driving in. I was like, 'Oh, I remember driving in' and you could feel the energy. But my time is over and to be able to sit back and look at the lives that I was able to touch, and to see the guys I used to play with, it's special.

"This is when all that hard work—when you're in the moment sometimes you don't want to get up and make those extra catches after practice. But anybody who's out there playing sports, whether it's football—I don't care what sport it is—it's worth it to put football at the top of your list and make it the most important thing in your life because it's given me everything. Doesn't mean that other stuff wasn't important to me, it's just that football, I always had that love and passion for it. And if I didn't have that I wouldn't be standing here with you guys."

Kansas City Chiefs tight end Tony Gonzalez dunks the ball over the goal post after scoring a touchdown against the Buffalo Bills on Nov. 23, 2008, at Arrowhead Stadium. (WD/Icon Sportswire)

For 12 seasons with the Chiefs, Gonzalez ran routes like a wide receiver, blocked like an offensive lineman and dunked the ball over the goalpost after scoring a touchdown. Gonzalez is the Chiefs' all-time leader in receptions (916), receiving yards (10,940), receiving touchdowns (76) and 100-yard receiving games (26). He made 10 straight Pro Bowls and was an All-Pro six times with the Chiefs.

"Anybody who's gone through what I've gone through—I don't care if you had the type of career that I had or if you're in the league a couple years—it's a family experience," Gonzalez said. "It's a family environment you create with the guys you played with and with your real family. So it's been great and I'm pinching myself. I get to go out and look up and see these fans and see my name in that Ring of Honor now with Len Dawson, Bobby Bell and Derrick Thomas. It's overwhelming and I'm blessed."

The Chiefs moved up five spots in the 1997 draft to get Gonzalez, who was a two-sport star at Cal, where he also played power forward on the basketball team. At 6-foot-5 and 250 pounds, Gonzalez had the size and athletic ability to dominant as a tight end position, but he possibly could have played in the NBA as well.

In 2002, the Chiefs placed the franchise tag on Gonzalez, and in the midst of a contract dispute he played basketball that summer for the Miami Heat. That July, Chiefs general manager Carl Peterson rescinded a long-term contract offer to Gonzalez until he gave up his hoop dreams for good.

Two months later, the Chiefs and Gonzalez agreed to a seven-year deal worth $31 million that included a $10 million signing bonus. The contract was the richest for a tight end in NFL history at the time. But Gonzalez never found playoff success with the Chiefs and requested a trade in 2008.

No trade was made then, as Peterson was not going to be retained the next season. So when the new regime of Scott Pioli came in, trade talks heated up. In April 2009, Gonzalez was dealt to Atlanta for a second-round pick.

Gonzalez played the next five seasons with the Falcons before retiring after the 2013 season. In all, he played 17 years and ranks second in NFL history with 1,325 receptions, trailing only Jerry Rice. Though Gonzalez has no intention to make a comeback, he wonders what he could have done if he played for the Chiefs today.

"I'd have loved it," Gonzalez said. "To be in an offense like this in this day and age with the rules the way they are, and to play with a guy like Patrick Mahomes, you just salivate. You're like, 'Man I wish I could do that.' I'm that crusty old guy saying, 'You know what I would have done if I would have been in this offense?' Take a guy like Travis Kelce, phenomenal athlete, unbelievable talent, and he's doing what he's supposed to be doing in this offense. He's setting records. I know he needed 100 yards to break my all-time record for a season, and I hope he gets it.

"Records are made to be broken. I got to break them, and now it's up to somebody else, and that's what you're going to see. I think all these quarterbacks throughout history are going to see these numbers start to fall because of this day and age of playing in the NFL, and I think it's great. Ratings are up, people love it. I love it. Obviously I'm an offensive guy, and I'm a little biased, but I love the way the NFL is trending up right now. It's a fun place to be."

Kansas City Chiefs tight end Travis Kelce spikes the ball in the end zone after scoring a touchdown against the Denver Broncos on October 28, 2018, at Arrowhead Stadium in Kansas City, Mo. (William Purnell/Icon Sportswire)

Travis Kelce

When Travis Kelce first met Andy Reid, he thought the Chiefs coach seemed congenial enough. That was after a University of Cincinnati-Temple football game in Philadelphia, where Reid was coach of the Eagles for 14 seasons.

The two didn't chat long, just enough to exchange pleasantries. The next time Reid talked to Kelce, the conversation turned out to be something the Chiefs tight end will always remember. It was April 26, 2013. Draft day.

The Chiefs selected tackle Eric Fisher with first overall pick the night before, and as Kelce's phone rang during the third round, a Missouri phone number popped up. Kelce immediately feared that it was the St. Louis Rams—a team he didn't really want to play for. Kelce answered the phone somewhat begrudgingly even though it was the call he had been waiting his whole life for.

On the other end, the voice he heard was not the one he expected. It was a familiar voice, but one he hadn't heard in months. It was Reid with an urgent question.

"Are you going to fuck this up?" Reid asked.

Kelce instantly was taken aback as his mind swirled. The Chiefs were the last team he expected to get a call from because they didn't show any interest in him during the weeks leading up to the draft. Kelce knew of the Chiefs, and that Kansas City had a fine reputation for barbecue. But that was pretty much it.

So as he listened to Reid explain what he expected from his players and the commitment level they must have to play for him, Kelce's heart skipped a beat. He was relieved it wasn't the Rams, and though he was being grilled by Reid, in that moment there was a sense of comfort.

Kelce's brother, Jason, played center for Reid with the Eagles, and his brother often spoke glowingly of the head coach. So in a matter of moments,

Kelce, who was already known for being a unique character and difficult to handle in college, had a decision to make. Could he adhere to Reid's lofty standards or should he pass and hope another team calls?

"All right, just give me a chance," Kelce told Reid.

The Chiefs selected Kelce with the 63rd overall pick, and he has since gone from backup to the best tight end in football. Kelce's journey has not been one without bumps in the road, but he has been allowed to be himself. And he and the Chiefs have found a way to coexist quite beautifully.

Catching Kelce

Kelce grew up in Cleveland Heights, Ohio, and was a standout quarterback in high school. He got a scholarship offer from Cincinnati and followed his brother there. Jason at that time was a starting offensive lineman for the Bearcats and the younger Kelce was a redshirt quarterback.

Kelce, however, lost his scholarship after he failed a drug test and was suspended from the team. He later moved in with his brother, sleeping on the floor and doing odd jobs for a year. Cincinnati then agreed to let Kelce back on the team as a walk-on if he moved to tight end where his 6-foot-5, 260-pound frame was a better fit.

Kelce agreed and eventually earned his scholarship back. The next year he caught 45 passes for 722 yards and eight touchdowns and emerged as one of the country's best prospects at his position. Coming off a disastrous 2-14 season, the Chiefs had holes everywhere, and Reid thought Kelce would be a perfect fit for his offense.

A knee injury limited Kelce to one game as a rookie, but his career take off the next, catching 67 passes for 862 yards and five touchdowns. In 2015, Kelce made the first of four straight Pro Bowls. In 2016, he had his own reality TV show, "Catching Kelce," which aired for one season on E!

While Kelce excelled at catching the football, reeling in the woman of his dreams proved rather difficult so the cameras chronicled his quest for true love. Initially 50 women competed for his affection, and with any good TV show, there's usually some drama. And that has been the case with Kelce at times during his career.

Paying the price

Kelce wears his heart on his sleeves and is a fiery competitor. Sometimes that's not exactly the best combination. In 2016 against the Jaguars, Kelce was thrown out of the game in the fourth quarter for throwing a towel at an official.

He was upset that a pass interference penalty wasn't called on a pass intended for him in the end zone. After Kelce argued with the referee to no avail, he threw his arms up and stormed off only to come back later and throw a towel that was tucked into his pants at the referee. Kelce was fined $25,000 for the incident.

Kelce has paid thousands in fines over the years. After the Chiefs' home playoff loss to the Steelers in January 2017, he was fined a combined $21,000 for punching a Steelers player after a play was over and for criticizing an official after the game.

On a critical two-point conversion late in the fourth quarter, a referee flagged Fisher for holding, a call that wiped out the game-tying conversion. The penalty was questionable at best, but Kelce was so incensed that he could only see the black and what stripes of the official.

"That was horseshit! This sucks!!" Kelce shouted in the Chiefs locker room after the game. "(He) shouldn't be able to wear a zebra jersey ever again! He shouldn't be able to work at fucking Footlocker!"

In 2017, Kelce's antics continued for a while. In the Chiefs' season opener at New England, he was flagged for a personal foul after shoving the ball into the midsection of a Patriots linebacker. A week later in the Chiefs' home opener against Philadelphia, he was called for taunting Eagles players on their sideline after Kareem Hunt scored on a 53-yard run.

A furious Reid barked at him, and Kelce sort of redeemed himself—at least momentarily in the eyes of Chiefs fans—by vaulting himself through the air from the 5-yard line to score the go-ahead touchdown in the fourth quarter.

"Well, I failed to hurdle a guy two plays before that so I just dusted myself off and tried it again," Kelce said after the game.

Kelce's flying leap might have been the highlight of his season, and it made quite an impression on his teammates.

"That was crazy," said then-Chiefs quarterback Alex Smith.

But perhaps crazier yet was what Kelce did after scoring the touchdown. He flapped his arms and mocked the Eagles' "Fly Eagles Fly" touchdown celebration. When asked about the penalty, Kelce didn't answer the question. He just offered this instead.

"Kareem Hunt went to the house, man," Kelce said. "He can play some football, I'll tell you that. And the O-line blocked it perfectly up front."

However, after another talking to by Reid, Kelce started to show more maturity as the season went along.

"The thing with Travis is he loves to play the game, and he's very competitive," Reid said. "He's knows he's going to get their best challenge every week. He's got to fight through some things. They try to double him, and grab him, and snag him, all those things. And so he understands that now I think.

"The more he's around it and kind of understands who he is and his perception to other teams, I think the better he understands he has to keep everything right."

In 2018, Kelce did that and more as he enjoyed a record-setting season. His 103 receptions were the most by a Chief in a single season. For a short time, his

1,336 yards receiving were the most in a season by a tight end in NFL history, but the record stood for less than an hour as San Francisco's George Kittle passed him at the close of Week 17.

Kelce, though, thanked his coaches and teammates—especially Patrick Mahomes—for putting together a season to remember.

"I'm just appreciative of him," Kelce said. "Him, Coach Reid, the offensive staff, everyone on the offensive line, the receivers. Like I said, it's the ultimate team game. So for me to be able to be accountable in there and up to that standard it means a lot to me. Next year I'll try to break whatever record is in my way."

Fellowship of the ring

In his first six seasons—five as a starter—Kelce has amassed 410 catches for 5,236 yards and 32 touchdowns, trailing only Tony Gonzalez on the team's all-time list for a tight end. It would be a tall task for Kelce to someday pass up Gonzalez, but with Mahomes at quarterback it possibly could be done. But there is another goal Kelce has his sights set on.

Kelce and his brother have always competed against each other whether it is in football, baseball or basketball. Now Travis wants what his brother has—a Super Bowl ring.

Jason was the Eagles' starting center in 2017 and helped lead the team to its first title in the Super Bowl era with a victory over the Patriots in Super Bowl LII. Kelce's former offensive coordinator with the Chiefs, Doug Pederson, guided the Eagles to the title in just his second season at the helm and that was an eye opener for Kelce.

"To go down that road even, it's more reachable," Kelce said of winning a Super Bowl in Kansas City. "I can get there because I've seen it done by guys with a similar offense and a similar team by guys that coached me.

"I got to take a secondhand look at the Eagles and I saw how tightknit of a group that was and they got a lot of guys to come together for one goal. And to live their lives focused on one goal, that's a powerful thing. And I think those guys all believed in each other and only had one goal in mind."

Kelce and the Chiefs share that same goal, and though it's been a bit of a bumpy ride at times, they wouldn't want him any other way.

"I try to go out there and perform on every single stage, no matter if it's practice or if it's out here in front of 80,000 or whoever is watching on their TV," Kelce said. "It's just going out there and being yourself, trying not to be anybody that you're not."

CHAPTER 10
OFFENSIVE LINE

Ed Budde

In 1963, the Chiefs had one of their best drafts as a franchise. That year they selected, defensive lineman Buck Buchanan first overall, left guard Ed Budde eighth overall and linebacker Bobby Bell in the seventh round of the AFL Draft. The team also selected punter Jerrell Wilson and fellow lineman David Hill, all of whom became starters on the Super Bowl teams.

The Eagles also selected Budde fourth overall in the NFL Draft and his contract offers were the same for both clubs. Budde picked the Chiefs partly due to his friendship with tight end Fred Arbanas.

Budde and Arbanas played together at Michigan State, and Arbanas raved to him about the exciting offenses in the new league that was about to begin its fourth season.

At 6-foot-5 and 260 pounds, Budde was a giant in his day. He also had a unique stance where instead of putting his right hand down, he put down his left. Budde was explosive off the snap and a punishing blocker.

On Oct. 20, 1968, the Chiefs upset the Raiders 24-10 with a depleted receiving corps, forcing them to run the ball almost exclusively. Len Dawson completed 2 of 3 passes that day for 16 yards while the Chiefs ran the ball 60 times for 294 yards and three touchdowns.

The Chiefs rushed for 215 yards in the first half, most of it running behind Budde and left tackle Jim Tyrer. Budde played so well that day that he was named the AFL's offensive player of the week, marking the first time in league history an interior offensive lineman received the honor.

"It's always the same formula, blocking and tackling," Chiefs coach Hank Stram said after the win. "We beat Oakland because of the sterling performance of Ed Budde and our entire offensive line. Budde's blocking at the point of attack was devastating."

The Chiefs lost to the Raiders in the playoffs that season but defeated them in the postseason the following year to advance to Super Bowl IV. The Chiefs-Raiders rivalry, however, remains strong with Budde.

"I've hated the Raiders since 1963," Budde once said. "It's a tradition that's been handed down over time."

Unfortunately for Budde another thing that's been handed down was the stigma that the AFL was largely made up of second-tier players. Even back-to-back Super Bowl titles by the Jets and Chiefs did little to change that perception by many Hall of Fame voters.

"One of the guys that I can't figure out is Ed Budde," said Rick Gosselin. "He was on the all-time All-AFL team and he's never gotten a sniff."

Meanwhile, Bills guard Billy Shaw, who was named to the AFL all-time team with Budde, has been in the Hall of Fame since 1999. Budde, who was a seven-time Pro Bowler and two-time All-Pro, retired in 1976 and was inducted into the Chiefs Hall of Fame in 1983.

Jack Rudnay

Playing in the Super Bowl is pretty much the only thing Jack Rudnay didn't do during his time with the Chiefs.

While Rudnay was there for Super Bowl IV, standing behind Hank Stram on the sidelines, the rookie center missed the entire 1969 season after suffering three broken vertebrae in his neck during a scrimmage for the College All-Star game.

Rudnay, though, quickly made a big impact on the Chiefs franchise once he was healthy. Selected in the fourth round of the 1969 draft out of Northwestern, Rudnay replaced Super Bowl starter E.J. Holub at center midway through the 1970 season.

From that point forward, Rudnay became one of the most dominant and durable players in the NFL for more than a decade. By the time he retired at the end of the 1982 season, Rudnay played in 178 games, including 144 straight, a streak that ran from 1970 to 1980.

Nicknamed "Joker" for his for his pranks on teammates, Rudnay was very intense on the football field. At 6-foot-2 and 240 pounds, he was undersized but his hard-nosed play meshed well with fellow linemen Ed Budde, Jim Tyrer and Dave Hill.

"The second effort is always there," Marv Levy once said about Rudnay.

From 1973-76, Rudnay made four straight trips to the Pro Bowl and in 1973 he was named the NFL's top center by the Associated Press. Rudnay also was voted team captain nine times and was a four-time All-Pro (1973-75, '79).

As the team got older and many of the Super Bowl players retired, Rudnay was one of the few bright spots on the team during from the late '70s and early

'80s. For as talented as Rudnay was, he played in just one playoff game during his Chiefs career, the 1971 double overtime loss to the Dolphins on Christmas.

"When I started playing football I learned it as a team sport, and that's what it still is," Rudnay told reporters after his last game. "You have to play together to be successful and to get anything out of the experience.

"I always thought of performance in relation to the team. Personal statistics don't mean a thing. The bottom line is what the team does."

Rudnay was inducted into the Chiefs Hall of Fame in 1994.

John Alt

One of the best players to ever wear the red and gold, John Alt's name is on the Ring of Honor at Arrowhead Stadium right next to Derrick Thomas.'

When Alt retired before the 1997 season, Thomas said he was the best tackle he had ever faced.

"In eight seasons I've faced almost every tackle in the National Football League and I've beaten them all," Thomas said. "But in eight years of practice and scrimmage I can only remember beating John Alt once. I think that is the highest compliment I can pay John."

Alt's 6-foot-8, 300-pound frame and No. 76 jersey was an imposing presence for the Chiefs. He was a Pro Bowler in 1992 and 1993 but battled knee, back and neck problems for most of his career until finally he could endure no more.

"There'll always be a part of me that wants to play," Alt said. "But I made a commitment to myself and my family a long time ago that I did not want to stick around when I thought my skills were diminished. I didn't want to be someone who hung on and hung on and hung on."

Alt was born in Germany, went to high school in Minnesota and played collegiately at Iowa. The Chiefs took him in the first round of the 1984 draft, but he struggled the first few years of his career. But once Marty Schottenheimer started walking the sidelines, Alt quickly became one of the best tackles in the game.

"As a coach, it's very, very important that you can rely on an individual's ability to play to a certain level all the time," an emotional Schottenheimer said at Alt's retirement news conference. "That is the thing I will always remember about John. You never worried about left tackle. He was the standard bearer."

Alt also left a mark on his teammates, especially center Tim Grunhard and left guard Dave Szott. Grunhard and Szott were drafted by the Chiefs in 1990 and played with Alt for seven seasons.

"By watching his work ethic, by watching the kind of things that he does, he made every one of us a better player," Grunhard said.

At Alt's retirement news conference, Grunhard and Szott made a David Letterman-style Top 10 list of reasons Alt was retiring. Among them were "His 14-year-old dog was dragging him on his daily jogs" and "John ran out of places to put braces on."

Alt, who spent his entire career with the Chiefs, was inducted into the team's Hall of Fame in 2002. He played in 10 playoff games with the team but his favorite game was a 21-7 victory in October 1995 at Denver. The Chiefs won in a blizzard.

"That one was the most fun I ever had," Alt said. "The snow let all the slow guys catch up with the fast guys. I did a belly slide after that game."

Will Shields

From 1993-2006 Will Shields played right guard for the Chiefs and played it better than anyone in the NFL.

Shields, who made 12 straight Pro Bowls and was an eight-time All-Pro, cleared the way for Marcus Allen, Priest Holmes and Larry Johnson. He also protected Joe Montana and Trent Green.

The son of a military man, Shields was born in Fort Riley, Kan., and grew up in Lawton, Okla. He sang in the choir as a kid and loved football. He played collegiately at Nebraska and won the Outland Trophy his senior year. At 6-foot-3 and 315 pounds, Shields wasn't the biggest lineman around but he was one of the most athletic, showing great ability to pull across the line of scrimmage and block down field.

Prior to the 1993 draft, the Chief sent a first-round pick to the 49ers for Montana and they used their-second round pick on Darren Mickell in the supplemental draft the previous year. That left the Chiefs with no pick until the third round. On draft day, general manager Carl Peterson was ecstatic to see Shields still on the board when the Chiefs were finally on the clock.

Peterson wasted little time in selecting Shields, knowing the top priority was to protect Montana, who he described as the organization's "porcelain doll." But not everyone was pleased with the pick. Then-offensive line coach Gary Gibbs told the media he wasn't sure if Shields could pass block since he played for the run-heavy Cornhuskers.

A firing mad Tom Osborne saw Gibbs' quotes in the paper and the Nebraska coach immediately called Peterson, whom he had known for years. Osborne was adamant that Shields could pass block quite well—something

Peterson already knew from having watched Shields play in person when he was in Lincoln.

Gibbs got an earful from Peterson, and after the dust settled, Shields quickly showed he was ready for the NFL. Gibbs also was opposed to starting rookies, so when Montana took the field for the season opener at Tampa Bay, Shields watched from the sideline.

In the first half, left guard Dave Szott went out with an injury and that opened the door for Shields. Right guard Danny Villa moved to the left side, and Shields took over at right guard and stayed there for the rest of his career—except for one game in 2000 when he moved to left tackle because the Chiefs were out of tackles due to injuries.

Quiet by nature, Shields often took naps in the locker room before games. On the field, he was extremely intelligent. In 14 seasons, Shields was flagged for holding just seven times and none during his last six seasons.

In the 1990s, John Alt, Szott, Tim Grunhard and Shields formed the best offensive line in football. In the early 2000s, that torch was passed to the line of Willie Roaf, Brian Waters, Casey Wiegmann, Shields and John Tait.

For his career, Shields played in 224 games and started 223 straight—both franchise records. He was named to the NFL's All-Decade team of the 2000s and was inducted into the Chiefs Hall of Fame in 2012. In 2015, he was enshrined in the Pro Football Hall of Fame.

"It's an honor being named into the Hall of Fame, to having those 10 letters added to your name," Shields said. "But it takes more than just yourself. It takes a village of people. And with me, it was truly a village because no one gets to the top by themselves. Someone had to push, prod and pull me to the next level, help me walk through the tough steps and be forever grateful."

For all his accomplishments on the field, Shields might be most proud of what he's done off it. In 2003, he was named the NFL's Walter Payton Man of the Year, and for years he has operated the Will to Succeed Foundation—an organization that helps neglected women and children—and 68 Inside Sports—a fitness and athletic training center in Kansas City.

Since he retired, Shields has stuck to a healthier diet and has lost 50 pounds. He also works with area youth, trying to teach them to stay active and eat healthier at a young age. Shields also regularly attends Chiefs' functions and he was the guest of honor for the pregame drum ceremony for the playoff game against the Colts in January 2019.

Brian Waters

As the left guard on one of the greatest offensive lines in team history, Brian Waters helped the Chiefs offense set records. And this fall he will be inducted into the team's Hall of Fame on alumni weekend.

"I'd like to thank my family and all of my friends," Waters said at the Chiefs draft party in April. "If there is one place that I would definitely want to be recognized and given this honor (it'd be here). This is the greatest accomplishment in my career, and I appreciate being able to share this with each and every last one of you."

Waters spent 11 of his 13 seasons in the NFL in Kansas City. The Chiefs signed him in 2000 after he originally signed with the Cowboys as an undrafted free agent in 1999. Waters played collegiately at North Texas and was a tight end his first three years before moving to defensive end as a senior.

After signing with the Chiefs, Waters was sent to NFL Europe to learn how to play offensive line. He started eight games in 2001 and was a Pro Bowler and All-Pro in 2004 and 2005. Waters was selected to the Pro Bowl five times with the Chiefs, his last coming in 2010. Waters played one season with the Patriots and one with the Cowboys before retiring in 2013.

Waters played in 163 games with 149 starts with the Chiefs. Waters also was named the Walter Payton Man of the Year in 2009.

"Although he was undrafted coming out of college, Brian made the most of his opportunity here in Kansas City," Chiefs chairman Clark Hunt said. "And his work ethic, talent and toughness made him an undisputed leader on the field and in the locker room.

"Brian also has a tremendous heart of service, and his commitment to the Kansas City community earned him the prestigious Walter Payton Man of the Year award in 2009. We look forward to adding Brian's name to the Ring of Honor at Arrowhead this fall."

Willie Roaf

Though he played left tackle for only four seasons in a Chiefs uniform, Willie Roaf's dominance on the field at the end of his career helped solidify his place as one of the best offensive linemen in NFL history.

After spending his first nine seasons with New Orleans, a 2002 trade brought Roaf to Kansas City. Roaf tore his right ACL in 2001 and missed nine games that season. The following spring, the Saints sent Roaf to the Chiefs for a fourth-round pick.

He arrived with seven Pro Bowls on his resume and made the Pro Bowl each of his four seasons with the Chiefs. He was inducted into the Pro Football Hall of Fame in 2012.

"The Kansas City Chiefs organization gave me another chance to play football after suffering a serious knee injury," Roaf said during his enshrinement speech. "They were the only team that would really give me another chance to play, and I want to thank the Hunt family for bringing me to Kansas City, especially Lamar Hunt and Carl Peterson.

"I played on one of the best offensive lines in the league while I was in Kansas City, and we set the tone for the team every week."

Roaf protected Trent Green's blind side and opened holes for Priest Holmes. In 2003, Holmes set a then-NFL record for rushing touchdowns with 27. The Chiefs would even have the athletic 6-foot-5, 320-pound Roaf pull on the edge.

The Chiefs led the NFL in scoring Roaf's first two seasons with the team, and he was an All Pro in 2003 and 2004. In 2005, Roaf missed six games with a strained hamstring and retired before the start of training camp in July 2006.

Roaf was a first-round pick of the Saints in 1993, going eighth overall and the first offensive lineman taken in the draft. Roaf grew up in Arkansas and Louisiana and was a highly-recruited basketball player in high school. But only two schools wanted him to play football—Louisiana Tech and Arkansas State. Roaf picked Louisiana Tech, the same school Terry Bradshaw went to.

Roaf played right tackle as a rookie in the NFL before moving to left tackle his second year. Roaf was an All-Pro seven times and is a member of the NFL's All-Decade team of the 1990s and 2000s.

CHAPTER 11
DEFENSIVE LINE

Buck Buchanan

Battling in the trenches wasn't something 6-foot-7, 285-pounders did in the 1960s and '70s. Men of that size were usually stationed at defensive end.

Buck Buchanan likely would have done fine on the edge had he stayed there as he also had the speed to run sideline to sideline and make tackles. But that's what made him so great as a right defensive tackle and Pro Football Hall of Famer for the Chiefs.

"Buck had it all," Chiefs coach Hank Stram once said. "Big, strong, fast and quick, plus he had a great attitude."

As a rookie in 1963, the Chiefs briefly tried him out at defensive end before moving him a few feet in. With his size, strength, speed—10.2 in the 100 yard dash—and determination, Buchanan revolutionized pass defense in the NFL. Offensive linemen couldn't guard him without help, and he became the first athletic big man who could pressure the quarterback from the interior.

For 13 seasons Buchanan helped lead the Chiefs defense—one that dominated the AFL from 1966 to 1971. The Chiefs went 64-23-4 in that stretch and played in Super Bowls I and IV as Buchanan, Curly Culp, Jerry Mays and Aaron Brown dominated the line of scrimmage in Stram's triple-stack defense.

Born Junious "Buck" Buchanan on Sept. 10, 1940, in Gainesville, Ala., Buchanan played football and basketball at Parker High School in Birmingham. The son of a millworker, Buchanan received no scholarship offers in either sport so one day his uncle called Grambling coach Eddie Robinson and told him he should give his nephew a look.

Robinson, like most coaches, was a little hesitant to take recruiting advice from a player's relatives but there was something about Buchanan that intrigued him. The next day Robinson called the school's principal and offered Buchanan a scholarship without ever watching him on tape. Buchanan went on to become an All-American, and Robinson once called him "the finest lineman I have seen."

The Dallas Texans, who would soon move to Kansas City and become the Chiefs, signed quarterback Len Dawson in 1962 and traded quarterback Cotton Davidson to the Raiders for a first-round pick. The Texans used that pick to take Buchanan first overall in the draft, and he signed with the club just minutes after being selected.

"I signed with them because I considered it an honor to be the first player chosen by the league," Buchanan once said. "I thought it was very significant to have that honor, since I had played for a small black school. I was determined to prove that players from small schools could play in the big leagues."

Buchanan anchored the defensive line, playing in six AFL All-Star games and the Pro Bowl twice. He also was remarkably durable, playing in all of the team's 182 regular season games during his career.

Buchanan also recorded the first sack in Super Bowl history, leaping onto the back of Packers quarterback Bart Starr in the first quarter of Super Bowl I and throwing him for a 7-yard loss. In Super Bowl IV against the Vikings, Buchanan sacked quarterback Joe Kapp for an 8-yard loss in the second quarter, and the Chiefs defense forced five turnovers in the win.

Buchanan retired after the 1975 season and in 1976 he became a defensive line coach for Stram in New Orleans. In 1978 he served as an assistant coach with the Browns before returning to Kansas City to start a restaurant. He later opened an advertising and construction business.

Buchanan was inducted into the Chiefs Hall of Fame in 1981 and in 1990 he was inducted into the Pro Football hall of Fame in Canton, Ohio. A few days before the ceremony, Buchanan was diagnosed with lung cancer and he died on July 16, 1992, at age 51.

"It's a big loss for the whole sports world, a major loss for Kansas City as a community," Lamar Hunt said after Buchanan's death. "He touched so many people in so many ways."

In 1995, the Buck Buchanan award was established. It honors the most outstanding defensive player in Division I FCS.

Curley Culp

Nose to nose, Curley Culp was a game-changer. And as one of the strongest men to ever play in the NFL, he revolutionized the nose tackle position and muscled his way to the Hall of Fame.

For seven seasons (1968-1974), Culp helped anchor the defensive line for the Kansas City Chiefs, proving to be the final piece for one of the NFL's greatest defenses. Culp was selected by Denver in the second round of the 1968 AFL Draft, but at 6-foot-2 and 265 pounds the Broncos believed he was a bit too small for the defensive line so they tried him out at guard before eventually trading him to the Chiefs for a fourth-round pick.

As a rookie, Culp helped lead the Chiefs to a 12-2 record, but they ultimately lost to the Raiders in the playoffs. A year later, the Chiefs defeated the Raiders in the final AFL championship game 17-7 as Culp had six tackles and a sack, helping lead the Chiefs to Super Bowl IV.

In the Super Bowl against the Vikings, Chiefs coach Hank Stram had another ingenious idea. In his triple-stack defense, the Chiefs played a 4-3. But in Super Bowl IV, Stram had Culp slide down from his defensive tackle position and line straight up over Vikings Pro Bowl center Mick Tingelhoff. This created a mismatch as Tingelhoff couldn't get to the second level, which freed up lanes for Buck Buchanan, Willie Lanier and Bobby Bell.

The Chiefs defense yielded only 67 yards rushing and Vikings quarterback Joe Kapp was under constant pressure. He was sacked three times and threw two interceptions as the Chiefs cruised to victory.

"In my second year of pro ball, going to the Super Bowl, that was kind of neat," Culp told the Kansas City Star. "It was awesome. Super Bowl IV was the last year of the AFL and we felt we could compete. We were underdogs. We knew they were going to try to run the ball against us, and we could stop them and force Joe Kapp to throw the ball. It worked out."

Moving Culp to the nose tackle position also began a wave of NFL teams implementing the 3-4 defense in the 1970s. The 3-4 scheme was already visible on the college level, and Culp already had plenty of experience playing nose tackle at Arizona State.

He was a standout at wrestler in high school and in 1967 he won the NCAA heavyweight championship at Arizona State. Culp went 84-11-1 as a wrestler at ASU and was a three-time Western Athletic Conference champion. In the 1967 NCAA tourney, he pinned three of his four opponents, leading the Sun Devils to the team title.

In 1974, Culp's contract with the Chiefs was set to expire so he signed a future contract with the Southern California Sun of the short-lived World Football League. The Chiefs then traded Culp—a two-time Pro Bowler—to the Houston Oilers four games into the season.

Culp spent parts of seven seasons with the Oilers and made the Pro Bowl four more times. He had hopes of returning to the Super Bowl, but the Oilers were defeated by the Pittsburgh Steelers in the AFC title game in 1978 and 1979.

He finished his career playing for the Detroit Lions in 1980 and 1981. Culp was inducted into the Chiefs Hall of Fame in 2008 and the Pro Football Hall of Fame in 2013.

"Curley was one of many great players that helped lead this franchise to a Super Bowl victory in 1970, and that team, including Curley, helped build the tradition and foundation of the Kansas City Chiefs," Chiefs chairman Clark Hunt said.

Neil Smith

The Chiefs have had major issues with the NFL salary cap at times over the years, and the day Neil Smith was told he wouldn't be part of the team's future, his heart broke.

Smith played left defensive end for the Chiefs from 1988 to 1996, and along with his close friend, the late, great Derrick Thomas, they terrorized quarterbacks and were the most successful sack duo of the '90s.

Smith and Thomas also built an unbreakable bond, and early in their careers they founded the Derrick Thomas/Neil Smith Third and Long Foundation with the goal to "sack childhood illiteracy" as both Thomas and Smith had dyslexia when they were kids.

Kansas City defensive end Neil Smith celebrates after sacking Brett Favre of the Green Bay Packers on Nov. 8, 1993, at Arrowhead Stadium. Smith played nine seasons with the Chiefs, but won two Super Bowls with the Broncos. (Kenneth Spencer Research Library, University of Kansas Libraries)

Smith was vocal about wanting to end his career with the Chiefs, but they decided to spend money on re-signing Thomas and signing free agent quarterback Elvis Grbac in March 1997. Marty Schottenheimer met with Smith in early April and told him that the team wouldn't be able to keep him.

"When I first came here I thought that I would end my career here in Kansas City," Smith said at news conference announcing his departure from Kansas City. "I would love to end my career here but it was a business decision that was made for the Kansas City Chiefs. I would have to say that I have to live with it. I'm big enough and old enough to handle it."

Smith was the second overall pick in the 1988 draft out of Nebraska. As a rookie, he struggled at times and some considered him a bust. That perception changed when the old regime was replaced with the arrival of Schottenheimer and Carl Peterson the following year.

The Chiefs had the fourth pick in the 1989 draft and believed if they added another pass rusher on the other side to complement Smith, he would flourish. And when Kansas City selected Thomas, it marked the beginning of a decade of dominance for the Chiefs defense.

In 1991, Smith earned the first of five consecutive trips to the Pro Bowl, making his patented "home-run swing" after a sack a nationwide hit. The gesture had local roots, though, as it honored Kansas City Royals legend and baseball Hall of Famer George Brett, who hit 317 home runs in his career. While Brett was one of the game's most prolific power hitters, Smith also had a reputation for being one of those in the NFL.

In 1994, the Chiefs played the 49ers at Arrowhead Stadium. The Chiefs won 24-17, sacking Steve Young four times. Thomas had three sacks, but in his autobiography "*QB: My Life Behind the Spiral*," Young wrote the hardest hit might have been from Smith, who blindsided him with "such force, that the wind is knocked out of me before I hit the ground. Gasping for air, I writhe in pain."

Smith led the NFL with 15 sacks in 1993 and led the team in 1994 (11) and 1995 (12). In 1996, Smith's production declined and he recorded just six sacks and at age 31 the Chiefs decided to go in a different direction.

"It was hard for me," Smith said. "A very emotional moment, sitting talking to Marty. I was hurt, I was crushed. But those things happen."

A week after being dumped by the Chiefs, he signed an incentive-laden one-year deal with Denver. The signing was made possible when John Elway restructured his contact so the Broncos could squeeze Smith in under the salary cap.

Smith went on to have a Pro Bowl season with the Broncos and helped them win two straight Super Bowls—a real gut-punch to Chiefs fans. Smith played one more season in Denver before finishing his career in San Diego.

After he retired, Smith returned to Kansas City and has remained active in the community. He is carrying Thomas' torch for the Third and Long Foundation, which provides youth mentoring programs and scholarships to any institution of higher learning.

Smith ended his Chiefs career with 89.5 career sacks, which at the time was second on the team's all-time list. He has since been passed by Tamba Hali.

"I have so many great memories both on the field and off the field," Smith said. "If I would just start getting into football plays and players and coaches and thigs I've done on the field and off the field, I could be here all day."

Chris Jones

For decades in the NFL it was believed that the quickest way to get to the quarterback was to rush from the outside. For the Chiefs, that philosophy seems to be changing.

With all the shotgun offenses and quick passes in the league today, the Chiefs are starting to believe that the fastest way to the QB might be up the middle—especially since they have Chris Jones.

One of the most talented and versatile defensive linemen in the NFL, and easily one of the most likable, the often hilarious Jones has quickly become a fan favorite in Kansas City. When Jones isn't wrapping up quarterbacks in the backfield, which isn't often, considering he had 15.5 sacks in 2018, he's usually joking around in the locker room.

Take, for instance, his first career interception in 2017. The Chiefs were playing the Eagles in Week 2 at Arrowhead Stadium and the score was tied 13-13 with nine minutes to go in the fourth quarter. Carson Wentz took a shotgun snap and under pressure threw a pass that bounced off Justin Houston's helmet. The ball went high into the air, and when Jones came down with it, he immediately ran backward, trying to cut across the middle and get to the sideline so he could take it to the end zone.

"I was headed home," Jones said. "I was out of here, man. I was thinking one of the little guys was about to kill me while I was jumping in the air this long. So that's why I backed up. I had to check out the scenery. I've seen Tyreek (Hill) do it too many times."

Thing is Hill has a knack for outrunning defenders, and Jones was pulled down by an Eagles offensive lineman after taking only a few steps.

Kansas City Chiefs defensive lineman Chris Jones (95) pumps up the crowd as the Chiefs take on the Chargers on Dec. 13, 2018, at Arrowhead Stadium. Jones had a career-high last season with 15.5 sacks. (William Purnell/Icon Sportswire)

"He didn't give me too much time to gather myself," Jones said, trying not to laugh. "It was a good interception, though."

Jones, a second-round pick in 2016 out of Mississippi State, started his career as a backup but worked his way into the rotation and started 11 games as a rookie. Jones recorded just two sacks his first season and tallied just 6.5 in his second year—three of those coming against the Eagles. Last offseason Jones, who is 6-foot-6 and at one point weighed 310 pounds, shed 25 pounds and crossed his fingers and hoped nobody would notice.

"That's why I'm wearing this jacket so nobody can see how small I actually am," Jones said. "You know, you got to have the figures. You *got* to have the figures. That was only for my purposes. I put myself on a strict diet. I tried to stay away from pork and everything and tried to be more of a veggie eater to try to last long in this game."

Though Jones has played just three seasons, he's only a few sacks away from cracking the team's top 10 in career sacks. Currently former linebacker Dee Ford ranks 10th with 30.5, and he and Jones had a bit of a friendly rivalry going last year.

When Ford was named the AFC Defensive Player of the Month in October, Jones took notice and delivered Ford a message that he would win the award the following month. Jones then recorded six sacks and four forced fumbles and won the award for November.

"It's just competiveness," Jones said. "I saw Dee win it and I'm like, 'I got to get me one, I got to get me one.' I went and told him, that I'm going to get this one this month, and he laughed at me, and I told him, 'Yep, it happened, huh?'"

Chiefs coach Andy Reid has seen Jones transform his game. Jones began his career clogging up the interior of the defensive line before shifting to end late in 2017.

Chiefs defensive lineman Chris Jones (95) sacks Los Angeles Chargers quarterback Philip Rivers on Dec. 13, 2018, in Kansas City, Mo. (Photo by Tom Walko/Icon Sportswire)

Jones responded by recording three sacks in his last four games that season but had to have offseason knee surgery—the second time in his NFL career. So Reid and the Chiefs decided that having Jones shed some weight to keep pressure off his knee, and playing him more on the outside would be best going forward. Jones then had the best season of his career and set an NFL record by recording a sack in 11 straight games in 2018.

Jones attributed his streak to a pair of lucky gloves that hadn't been washed, and according to him "smelled like a dead animal." Reid believes it was something else.

"You saw the change in his body, how he really took care of himself physically with diet and workouts and all that this offseason," Reid said. "His body fat's way down and then he works on his fundamentals and techniques, that's what he does. And he's still got room to grow, which is great. He's not tapped out by any means."

Jones believes Reid is right and that he still has more to give to the game—as an offensive player. In fact, Jones can see himself playing quarterback, running back and wide receiver for the Chiefs.

"I think it's about time we take the necessary steps as an organization to put Chris Jones back there," he jokingly said. "We only got one time to mess up so I'm going to make sure I go out there practicing throwing the ball to the receivers so when my number is called I'll be ready."

Jones was hoping to catch Patrick Mahomes' historic 31st touchdown pass last season but didn't get the chance. He did, however, find the end zone when he intercepted a pass against Jacksonville and ran 20 yards for a score, somewhat making up for the time he was tackled well short of the goal line on a play that kick-started his career the year before.

"I'm not really as vocal as everybody else. I'm a quiet guy," Jones said with a straight face before bursting into laughter. "I'm just playing with you! You know it!"

CHAPTER 12
LINEBACKERS

Bobby Bell

Before he left his boyhood home in North Carolina to play college football at Minnesota in 1959, Bobby Bell promised his dad that he would get his degree and graduate.

Bell made good on that promise—in May 2015 at age 74.

"I wish I had done it earlier but I didn't. But I'm glad I done it," a very proud Bell said after graduating from Minnesota's College of Education and Human Development with a degree in parks, recreation and leisure studies. "I don't know how to tell you the feeling."

Bell grew up in Shelby, and as a kid he wished he could play in the same swimming pools and recreation parks that the white kids did. But he couldn't because of the color of his skin.

Bell attended Cleveland High, a small all-black school that played six-man football until his senior year when an 11-man team was formed. He was a running back his first two seasons before moving to quarterback his junior year. Football was Bell's third-best sport as he also had a bright future playing baseball and basketball.

Bell's father, Pink, was a cotton mill worker who didn't graduate high school. His mother, Zannie, also wasn't well-educated, and they wanted their son to have more opportunities than they did. When Bell was 16, the Chicago White Sox offered him a minor league contract, but the dream of playing at a "big school" appealed to Bell and his family so he stayed in school and became an all-state quarterback.

Bell wanted to play college ball at North Carolina, but the school was segregated at the time. At a high school all-star game in Greensboro, Bell's play caught the attention of UNC coach Jim Tatum, who phoned Minnesota coach Murray Warmath and told him that Bell would make a great addition to his squad, which already had a few black players.

Intrigued, Warmath called the Cleveland High principal to see if he could get some game film of Bell. Warmath surely raised his brow when the principal told him he had never heard of something called "game film" and suggested he contact the Shelby newspaper, which he thought had taken a few photos of Bell during one of the games.

Despite never actually seeing any film of Bell, Warmath offered him a scholarship. Before Bell boarded a plane for the first time in his life, his father gave him a gold Bulova watch—a parting gift because he wanted his son to always be on time as a college kid playing football in Minneapolis.

The first time his father watched him play in college, Bell broke three ribs and had to be carried off the field on a stretcher. Pink walked down the tunnel into the locker room and told his son that he didn't travel all that way to not watch him play. So Bell got up off the table, ran back onto the field and put himself back in the game.

Bell began his college career as a quarterback before moving to tackle and defensive end as a sophomore in 1960. Led by Bell, Minnesota won the national championship that season. In 1961 and 1962, Bell was an All-American, winning the Outland Trophy on the way to finishing third for the Heisman his senior year.

As the nation's top defensive lineman, he made the rounds on late-night TV and was selected by the Chiefs in the seventh round of the AFL Draft. The

Vikings also picked him in the second round of the NFL Draft, but he signed with the Chiefs because they offered him $500 more.

Initially, Bell thought he might have made a mistake opting to play for Lamar Hunt. After he signed with the Chiefs, Bell and Hunt once shared a cab. When it came time to pay, Hunt asked Bell if he could pick up the tab as he had no cash on him.

Bell begrudgingly paid the 15 cents and for a minute he actually thought Hunt might be broke. Bell eventually got his money back years later. On his 60th birthday Hunt sent him a card. When he opened it 15 cents were taped to the inside.

In Bell's days, player salaries weren't near what they are today so he also worked full-time at the local General Motors plant and often had to use vacation time to attend team workouts before the season.

Bell played defensive tackle and left defensive end his first two years with the Chiefs, but at 6-foot-4 and 225 pounds, he was shaped like an inverted pyramid. He had broad shoulders, a 30-inch waist and could run a 4.5 40. So Hank Stram moved him to left outside linebacker and he became a perennial All-Pro.

Bell, one of the best all-around athletes in the game, was tough against the run, and he could rush the passer and drop back into coverage. He had 26 interceptions in his career and returned six for touchdowns. He was the team's long snapper and even played on kick returns. In fact, Stram was certain Bell could play any position on the field.

"I can honestly say that Bobby Bell had as much talent as anyone I ever coached," Stram once said.

Bell became the first outside linebacker and first Chiefs player inducted into the Pro Football Hall of Fame in 1983. After he retired nine years earlier, he opened a chain of barbecue restaurants in Kansas City and later became a motivational speaker.

With each year it seemed Bell got busier and time started to get away from him. He kept telling himself that next year he would take the plunge and finish his degree, but it wasn't until May 2014 when he finally re-enrolled.

Minnesota officials dug up Bell's transcript, which was more than 50 years old and written in pencil. It showed he was 13 credits shy of earning his degree. Bell took online courses and got a little help from his son, Bobby Jr., and a few people with Chiefs on how to use an iPad and make PowerPoint presentations.

For one of his classes, Bell oversaw a youth football camp at Pittsburg State, a Division II school in Pittsburg, Kan., where then-Gophers coach Jerry Kill got his start in coaching. At Bell's graduation he wore his Super Bowl ring, black cap and gown, and a proud smile the whole time. He also still had the watch his father gave him so long ago.

For five decades the watch served as a reminder of a father's love and an unfulfilled promise by a son. But when Bell walked across the stage with his degree in hand, he looked at the watch on his left wrist and thought of his father, who like his mother had passed away years ago. True to his word, Bell had finished the job. A lesson learned and a promise kept.

"My dad's up there saying, 'I told you, boy, you could do it,'" Bell said. "I finished. I had all kinds of stuff on the wall, all kinds of plaques. All-American this, Outland Trophy, (second) runner-up for the Heisman, All-Star, Pro Bowl, Super Bowl, won a high school championship, college national championship, Rose Bowl championship. You name it, I did them all. And then I get an opportunity to play in the NFL—pro football—and it just kept going.

"I've met five presidents, shook their hands. Been around the world, did USO shows, know famous people all over the world. Bob Hope became a good friend of mine. Ed Sullivan, I did his show twice. Johnny Carson, national TV all the time. What can I guy ask for?"

Willie Lanier

Of all the Chiefs greats of yesteryear, Willie Lanier might have had the best viewpoint of all. As the middle linebacker for one of the best defenses the game has ever seen, Lanier was surrounded by Hall of Fame talent and he fit right in.

In the huddle, Lanier called the plays and he also inspired his team. In the divisional round playoff game against the New York Jets on Dec. 20, 1969, the Chiefs squared off against Joe Namath and the defending champs on a cold, blustery day at Shea Stadium in New York. In the fourth quarter, the Chiefs led 6-3 but faced a difficult task—stopping the Jets from first-and-goal at the 1.

With the elements making it extremely difficult for the offenses, it was pretty much a given that the first touchdown scored would be the game-winner. So in the huddle, Lanier made a passionate, tearful plea to his teammates about the Jets' next three plays.

"They're not going to score! They're not going to score!" Lanier shouted.

The eight-time All-Pro was right. On first down, the Jets handed off to running back Matt Snell, who ran to the right but was stopped by Lanier for a gain of a half-yard. On second down, the Jets ran Bill Mathis up the middle only to be tackled by a flying Lanier for no gain.

On third down, Namath rolled to the right but was pressured by three Chiefs—linebackers Bobby Bell and Jim Lynch and defensive back Jim Kearney. Namath's pass fell incomplete, and the Jets were forced to settle for a game-tying field goal.

Fired up by the defensive stop, on the ensuing possession Len Dawson quickly drove the Chiefs down the field in two plays. He first connected with Otis Taylor for a 61-yard gain, and his 19-yard pass to Gloster Richardson in the end zone gave the Chiefs a 13-6 win.

A few weeks later in Super Bowl IV Lanier came up big again, recording seven tackles and an interception in the Chiefs' win over the Vikings—all of which would not have been possible if not for that goal-line stand against the Jets.

"It was his tears and determination that helped stop the Jets on what was the goal-line stand, the all-time goal-line stand in Chiefs history," Chiefs founder Lamar Hunt said at Lanier's induction into the Pro Football Hall of Fame in 1986.

From 1967-77 Lanier devoured opponents with his size, quickness, toughness and intelligence. Coming off a 35-10 loss to the Green Bay Packers in Super Bowl I, Hank Stram thought his team needed to be stronger up the middle.

With the first of the team's two-second round picks, Stram selected Lynch out of Notre Dame. A few picks later he selected Lanier, who starred at small-school Morgan State, an all-black college in Baltimore.

In training camp Lynch and Lanier were supposed to compete for the starting middle linebacker job, but Lynch missed the first couple weeks of practice as he was chosen to play in the college all-star game. By the time Lynch got to camp, Lanier had already taken the job, becoming the first African American to start at middle linebacker in the pros.

"We don't particularly care what color he is, what nationality, what anything," Stram said after Lanier was drafted. "The only concern we have is bringing him in with the idea of competing for our squad. And if they earn the right to be a member of our 40-man squad, then they're going to be here."

Early in Lanier's rookie season, opponents gave him the nickname "Contact" as was already well known for his big hits. Lanier's helmet also was custom-made. It featured a heavy-duty facemask and extra padding on the outside, made not for his protection but for others.

Lanier also led with the crown of his helmet, which would draw all sorts of fines and ejections today. In the fifth game of his rookie year, Lanier suffered a head injury when his helmet hit the knee of a Chargers running back. Lanier felt no pain and didn't say anything about it so he stayed in the game. The next week at home against Houston, Lanier collapsed while calling the defensive signals and was rushed to the hospital.

On the way there Lanier's pulse was lost three times—something team officials didn't tell him until after he retired. When Lanier returned to the field a few weeks after the injury, he changed his playing style and his nickname, going from "Contact" to "Honey Bear" as he began to use his shoulder pads and wrap up ball carriers with his arms in a big "bear hug" before driving them to the ground with his legs.

Tackles weren't an official statistic during Lanier's career but he did record 27 interceptions and only missed one game the last 10 seasons of his career. Lanier won the NFL's Man of the Year award in 1972 for his charity work and in 1985 he was inducted into the Chiefs Hall of Fame. In 1994, he was named one of the top 75 players in NFL history.

Since he retired, Lanier has found success in the business world as a financial advisor in his home state of Virginia. He even funded a $500,000 scholarship program to Morgan State. Lanier also stays involved with football. He gives speeches to youth and has served on the NFL's safety panel for several years.

The Chiefs drafted Derrick Thomas with the fourth overall pick in the 1989 NFL Draft. Thomas had 10 sacks that season and was named the NFL's Defensive Rookie of the Year. (Cliff Welch/Icon Sportswire)

Derrick Thomas

Prior to the 1989 NFL Draft, Carl Peterson sat down with Marty Schottenheimer. A tremendous opportunity to the turn the tide was right in front of them.

The Chiefs held the fourth overall pick in the draft, but as Peterson so often said during his tenure, "the draft is an inexact science." One thing was certain in his mind though, and no scientific experiment would be needed to prove its validity.

"Marty, if we're ever picking fourth again in the NFL Draft, you and I will be out," Peterson told him. "So let's get it right."

Leading up to the draft, the Chiefs were pretty sure the Cowboys were going to select Troy Aikman with the top pick and the Lions were going to take Wichita, Kan., native Barry Sanders with the second pick. The big question mark was Green Bay with the third pick, but the Packers selected offensive guard Tony Mandarich, much to the delight of the Chiefs.

Derrick Thomas is the one they wanted all along. The pass-rushing specialist from Alabama wowed the Chiefs on tape and when they worked him out in person in Tuscaloosa, Ala. It was hot and muggy that March day when Peterson, Schottenheimer and Bill Cowher set foot on Alabama's campus to get a closer look at Thomas.

Peterson had watched Thomas play earlier at an Alabama-Auburn game and talked to him at the NFL Combine a month before in Indianapolis. Thomas ran the 40-yard dash, but his agent advised him not to lift or go through any drills. Peterson wasn't happy about that, and with no workout to go by, the Chiefs had to fly south and go to Thomas' workout.

On the Astroturf at Bryant-Denny Stadium, Cowher, then a young defensive coordinator, readied to begin the workout. Before it started, Schottenheimer instructed him to work Thomas until he dropped.

Cowher began with a few linebacker drills, and a couple Alabama participants soon fell due to exhaustion. Thomas, meanwhile, kept going. Cowher went through every linebacker drill he could think of. Yet, there stood Thomas, smiling at the men in Chiefs attire.

"What else would you like to see?" Thomas asked them.

Schottenheimer instructed Cowher to run Thomas through the defensive line drills—all of them. Later, when Thomas still would not yield, Cowher went through every defensive back drill he knew. Again, Thomas looked over and smiled.

"What else would you like to see?" he asked.

The Chiefs had seen enough on that day, but three decades later fans still wish they could have had more time to watch Thomas play football, and see the sacks, safeties and fumbles. They also wish they could have had more time to watch him live life. It's been nearly 20 years since Thomas—one of the most beloved players in Chiefs history—died in a Miami hospital, sent there after being paralyzed from the chest down in a car accident on a snowy and ice-covered freeway in Kansas City.

His rise from wild child to NFL star was as fast as his first step off the line of scrimmage. His interest in his father's life and the assassination of a president took him all over the world and he dreamed of eradicating illiteracy as much as he dreamed of sacking quarterbacks.

With a lightning-quick first step Derrick Thomas was a nightmare for opposing tackles. Thomas is the Chiefs all-time leader in sacks with 126.5. (Kevin Reece/Icon Sportswire)

KC's cornerstone

The oldest of Edith Morgan's seven children, Thomas was born Jan. 1, 1967, in Miami. He was raised by his mother and her parents, but he ran with the wrong crowd as a kid. At first he stole bikes. Then breaking into houses and stealing cars became common for the 14-year-old.

A judge sent Thomas to Dade Marine Institute, a facility for troubled youths. Thomas, finally out of reach from the people he hung out with, began to make huge strides. He completed the six-month course in only a few months and returned to school at South Miami High. As a senior linebacker on the football team, he earned a scholarship from Alabama.

Thomas had 18 sacks as a junior for the Crimson Tide. As a senior he set the school's single-season record with 27, winning the Butkus award and becoming an All-American.

In 1989 with the Chiefs, Thomas recorded 10 sacks, made the first of nine straight Pro Bowls, and was named Defensive Rookie of the Year. Already nearly unblockable, his leverage, speed and power only grew from there. For the next decade when the Chiefs needed a big play on defense, every eye looked to Thomas.

In 1990, his career skyrocketed, recording 20 sacks and six forced fumbles. On Veteran's Day, Thomas set the NFL single-game record by sacking Seattle quarterback Dave Krieg seven times. His performance was inspired by his father, who was shot down in Vietnam when Derrick was only 5.

"I kept thinking my father was up there watching me," Thomas said after the game. "I wanted to make sure he was proud of me."

Thomas also had a knack for calling his shot. Three times in his career he predicted doom for the opposing quarterback and succeeded, one of them coming on his sack and safety of 49ers quarterback Steve Young in 1994.

In 1996, the Packers came to Arrowhead Stadium, and Thomas made a lasting impression on a young assistant coach named Andy Reid.

"We came down here and played the Chiefs," Reid said. "Thomas put (Don) Beebe in the fifth row on a shallow crossing route, and we were out of receivers."

That year the Packers went on to win the Super Bowl—something the Chiefs couldn't accomplish in Thomas' 11 seasons. Standing in the way, most notably, was John Elway.

Elway, however, greatly admired Thomas, the man who sacked him 17 times, including once in 1997 that marked the 100th sack of Thomas' career. When Thomas' career ended, he finished with 126.5 sacks, 41 forced fumbles, and 19 fumble recoveries, four of which he returned for touchdowns. All of those are team records.

Man on a mission

Each day young Derrick would look at the alarm clock near his bed. He would believe that in a few minutes his father, Air Force captain Robert Thomas, would return home safely from war. But eventually those minutes slowly turned into years.

Thomas didn't really know much about his father until he was a student at Alabama studying criminal justice. But in the years that followed he wanted to be just like him.

The last time Thomas saw his father was in 1972, not long after he turned 5. It was at an Air Force base in Del Rio, Texas, where Thomas kissed and hugged him goodbye.

On Dec. 18, 1972, his father was co-piloting a B-52 during Operation Linebacker II over North Vietnam. Shortly after dropping their bombs the aircraft was hit by enemy fire—a SAM missile. The pilot and gunner were killed instantly. Three other crewmen parachuted out and survived.

Thomas' father was the last one to jump and he was seen in the air just seconds before the plane exploded. His body was never found and he was declared legally dead in 1980.

Thomas had great admiration for the military. It was one way to connect him to his father. During his NFL career, Thomas would often visit Whiteman Air Force base in Missouri and spend time with the pilots. He'd even go for rides in the jets, which peaked his interest in taking flying lessons himself.

Sometimes before games the Chiefs would have B-52 flyovers at Arrowhead Stadium, and on those days Thomas would always play great. On the day he recorded seven sacks, Thomas wore a bandana that had fighter jets on it.

Besides planes, Thomas was fascinated with conspiracy theories in the assassination of John F. Kennedy. He also hung out with Michael Jordan and was big pals with country star Hank Williams Jr. Thomas also liked to throw parties, and he fathered seven children with five different women. He was seemingly always on the go, but he loved sitting down and helping kids learn to read.

In 1990, he and Neil Smith started the Third and Long Foundation. On Saturdays before home games, Thomas and other teammates, including Joe Montana and Marcus Allen, would read to the class of 58 students.

Thomas gave countless hours and millions of dollars to improving children's lives and in 1992 he was named one of President George H.W. Bush's 1,000 Points of Light. In 1993, he was the keynote speaker at the Vietnam Veterans Memorial in Washington and he was named the NFL's Man of the Year.

"I can't tell you how big my heart is," Thomas once said.

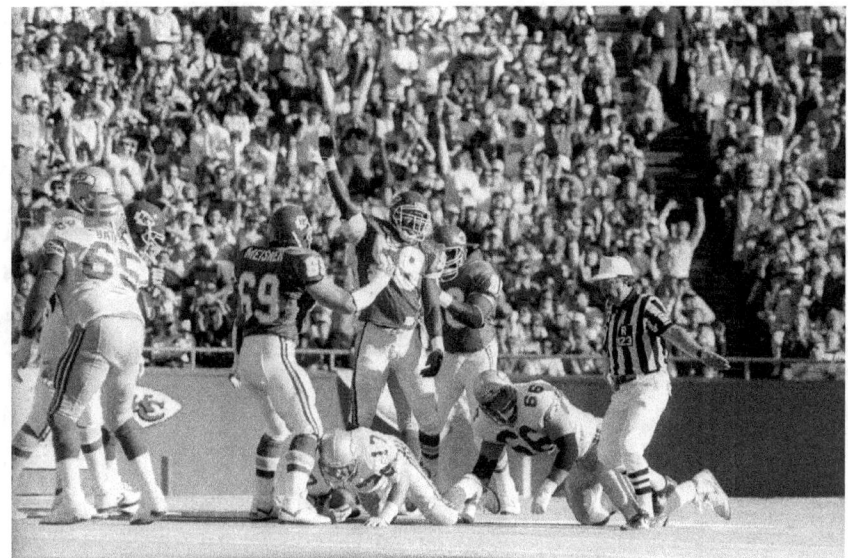

Derrick Thomas set the NFL record with seven sacks in a game against the Seattle Seahawks on Nov. 11, 1990, at Arrowhead Stadium. Here he is celebrating one of those sacks after pulling down Seattle quarterback Dave Krieg. (Kenneth Spencer Research Library, University of Kansas Libraries)

Losing a hero

Thomas lived life in the fast lane and was notoriously late for everything, especially team meetings. Coaches would frown at him when he'd slide into his seat just as they were about to begin. Thomas also was impulsive. On Jan. 23, 2000, he and two friends decided to go to St. Louis to watch the NFC championship game that Sunday afternoon between the Rams and Buccaneers.

In a rush to catch their plane, Thomas drove his 1999 Chevy Suburban 70 mph, way too fast for the icy conditions on I-435 in North Kansas City. The SUV slid off the road and flipped several times.

Thomas and friend Michael Tellis were not wearing seat belts and thrown from the car. Tellis died at the scene. A third passenger, John Hagenbusch, was wearing his seat belt and walked away from the crash.

Thomas was taken to Liberty Hospital with a broken neck and back. After he was stabilized he was transferred to Jackson Memorial Hospital, a leading trauma center for spinal-cord injuries in Miami.

Peterson, who Thomas considered a father figure, flew to Miami to visit him. So did Schottenheimer and Gunther Cunningham. Thomas was paralyzed from the chest down but slowly started to improve.

Doctors even became optimistic that he might walk again, which made the news of his death on Feb. 8 even more shocking. Peterson had just talked to him the day before.

"He was positive," Peterson said. "He was Derrick. He was in a wheelchair. I said, 'Son, you're mobile.' He said, 'Father, I am. I've got wheels.'"

As Thomas was being transferred from his bed to a wheelchair for more rehab, his eyes rolled back. He died from a pulmonary embolism, a blood clot in his legs traveled to his lungs. Back in Kansas City and across the country, fans, players and coaches grieved the loss of an icon who was just 33.

"It's hard for many of us to realize that even the strongest branch is easily broken," Schottenheimer said in a statement that day. "Derrick Thomas spent his entire professional career in Kansas City, and it was my good fortune to coach all of it but one year. Arriving in Kansas City as a young man of 22, he distinguished himself not only athletically, but as a giving and caring person."

Cunningham, who served as Thomas' defensive coordinator and head coach for a year, took the linebacker's death as hard as anyone.

"I looked at Derrick Thomas as one of the finest people I've ever been around, and a friend," Cunningham said. "Derrick will hang over this stadium forever."

Days later, thousands of Chiefs fans attended an open-casket viewing at Arrowhead Stadium, many of them wearing his No. 58 jersey. Funerals in Kansas City and Miami followed.

In 2001, Thomas was inducted into the Chiefs Hall of Fame. That same year the Chiefs renamed their Player of the Year award the Derrick Thomas award. In 2009, D.T. was finally enshrined in the Pro Football Hall of Fame, an appropriate final honor for a man who was a hero to many in so many different ways.

Tamba Hali

Tamba Hali began his career as a defensive end, but he will go down as one of the best pass rushers in Chiefs history as a linebacker.

Hali was drafted by Kansas City with the 20th pick in the first round of the 2006 draft out of Penn State. He played for the Chiefs for 12 seasons and in that time, Hali had many big hits on and off the football field as a football player, social media star and musician.

Hali's 89.5 sacks and 33 fumbles forced are both second-most in franchise history, trailing only Derrick Thomas. After recording 15.5 sacks his first two seasons as a defensive end, he recorded just three sacks his third year.

A little undersized on the line of scrimmage at 6-foot-2 and 265 pounds, Hali had a quick first step and relentless motor so a move to right outside linebacker in 2009 seemed natural. There he earned five straight trips to the Pro Bowl from 2011-15.

Hali was the focal point of the Chiefs defense during the height of his career before knee injuries slowed him down in his 30s. His playing time also decreased drastically his final two seasons, as he started just two games in 2016 and played in only five in 2017.

Late in the 2017 season, Hali was contemplating retirement and said the decision would be based on his family.

"All you think about is the family," Hali said. "I got four kids and this is great to be a Chief for 12 years. To get up and move somewhere else, it's not going to be based on anything but the family. I love playing, but they're the priority."

Tamba Hali began his career as a defensive end but switched to outside linebacker and made the Pro Bowl five times in 12 seasons with the Chiefs. (William Purnell/Icon Sportswire)

Two months later, his career with the Chiefs came to a close as he was released in March 2018. After his release, Hali, who is known for sharing his thoughts on Twitter, expressed his appreciation for the organization.

"I thank the greatest fans in the world #ChiefsKingdom for 12 incredible years," He tweeted. "I also want to thank the @Chiefs organization for believing in me from the beginning. All the support during my career in Kansas City has been overwhelming and #KC will always be special to me."

Hali grew up in Gbarnga, Liberia, and when he was 10 years old, he and his three brothers and sister fled to the United States to escape the country's civil war. When Hali reached the U.S. he met up with his father who was a chemistry professor in Teaneck, New Jersey.

Hali played football and basketball in high school and hoped he could one day make enough money to bring his mother to the U.S. Soon after he was drafted, the Chiefs and former-football-player-turned politician Jack Kemp wrote a letter to the immigration department in Liberia requesting that Hali's mother be able to leave the country and come to the U.S.

Liberia eventually agreed and on Oct. 1, 2006, Hali's mother watched her son record his first NFL sack by taking down 49ers quarterback Alex Smith.

In 2014, Hali donated $50,000 to help build an Ebola treatment center in Liberia as the deadly disease was spreading across his home country. In April 2016, he returned to his homeland for the first time since he left. He got to see his childhood home, go swimming and walk trails that used to be war zones.

Hali also shared photos and videos of his trip on his Instagram account, acknowledging how much progress the country has made with a simple post reading, "Liberian supporting Liberian, we've come a far way."

Tamba's tweets

Hali has always been popular on social media, but in July 2017—just a few days before training camp opened—he set off a firestorm with a Twitter rant. He vented frustrations for how little he was used in the team's home playoff loss to the Steelers six months earlier.

In the 18-16 loss to the Steelers, Hali played just seven snaps, and he tweeted, "Am I needed in KC anymore?" Hali also seemingly called out starters Eric Berry, Justin Houston and Marcus Peters for being absent for all 10 of the team's OTAs that May even though player attendance wasn't mandatory.

"I haven't missed any off-season workouts in 11 years w/the Chiefs," Hali tweeted. "Let's look at the Super Bowl champs I am sure they had 100% attendance for OTAS AND OFFFSEASON WORKOUT this year. I may be wrong."

Chiefs coach Andy Reid later addressed the matter as best he could.

"It is something as a coach that is out of your hands," Reid said. "Do you want everybody here? Sure, you want everybody here. But it is a voluntary camp. Tamba sounded like an angry coach there. He doesn't need to go there, he doesn't need to do all of that.

"Those guys understand Tamba. They know him better than anybody. Every team goes through this. Every team, there are guys there and not there because of the voluntary part of that. That is the rule and that is what it is and we go through it."

After Berry, Houston and Peters reported to mandatory minicamp in mid-June, the hullabaloo was largely over. Hali, however, wished he would have handled it better.

"I would probably do it a little bit different," he said. "I wouldn't be on Twitter doing it the way I did. I probably would have contacted Coach just to figure it out behind closed doors."

The music man

As a boy in Liberia, Hali played drums, bongos and sang in the church choir. Music has always helped guide him spiritually and culturally. Some of his favorite artists include Tupac, Jay-Z and the Notorious BIG.

While he was still playing, Hali began a side career as a rapper and producer and started his own record company in 2009. He signed a few artists and producers but has since downsized, focusing on his own music.

Hali's lyrics are positive-themed and they can hit close to home. The Chiefs would sometimes play his music in practice and during warmups, and in 2017 he released a single titled "Chief," a song dedicated to Chiefs fans.

"Marketing is going well," Hali said then. "People are taking heat to the music. It's really friendly. Dance music, African, bluegrass. But it's doing well. I'm surprised to see how much. I enjoy doing music so I will always do it."

In 2018, Hali released an EP titled "Tamba Juice."

Derrick Johnson

A better ending would have been fitting, one where Derrick Johnson spent his entire career in a Kansas City Chiefs uniform, and at least got to enjoy the thrill of a home playoff win at Arrowhead Stadium.

Johnson played linebacker for the Chiefs from 2005-17, and for those 13 seasons he gave everything he had to the city and organization. You could also make the case that he gave more to the Chiefs than they gave in return.

The NFL is a brutal business. Salary-cap casualties are routine transactions as veterans often clean out their lockers to make way for the next wave of young stars and Johnson played the 2017 season knowing that could be a possibility. Always putting the team first, Johnson even reworked his contract in March of that year to give the Chiefs some much-needed salary cap relief as free agency was starting and the NFL Draft was right around the corner.

There was one caveat, however. By agreeing to a new deal, Johnson was eligible for free agency a year early. So in February 2018, while Johnson and Chiefs fans were still smarting from the stunning home playoff loss to the Tennessee Titans just a month before, the bandage on the wound was ripped off too soon.

Johnson, a first-round pick and fan favorite from the start, was told he would not be brought back as the team looked to get younger on defense. In the weeks leading up to the decision, Johnson told Chiefs GM Brett Veach that he would take a pay cut to remain a Chief but the answer was still no.

Johnson ended his Chiefs' career as the team's all-time leading tackler with 1,262 stops. Blessed with good speed and quickness, he began his career as an outside linebacker before moving inside later on. Johnson had 27.5 sacks and 14 interceptions as a Chief and four of those picks he returned for a touchdown.

Kansas City Chiefs inside linebacker Derrick Johnson (56) puts a hard hit on Oakland Raiders running back Marshawn Lynch on Dec. 10, 2017, at Arrowhead Stadium. Johnson played 13 seasons with the Chiefs and is the team's all-time leading tackler. (Scott Winters/Icon Sportswire)

But for all the great plays Johnson gave, one of his best unfortunately stands out for the wrong reason.

The Forward Progress game

In the playoffs, the Chiefs have had a long history of being done in by kickers, defenses that can't stop anybody and yes, some bad calls that have gone against them. But following the team's loss to the Titans, Jeff Triplette and the other officials caught the ire of Chiefs fans for two calls that didn't go their way.

The first came with the Chiefs leading 14-0 late in the second quarter. On third down, Marcus Mariota dropped back to pass and Johnson blitzed up the middle. When Johnson's shoulder pads crashed into Mariota's chest, he fumbled the ball while in mid-air and linebacker Justin Houston scooped it up.

But a whistle had already blown the play dead, and Johnson's fumble was nullified because officials said Mariota's forward progress had been stopped. However, the replay clearly showed that the only forward progress that was stopped on that play was Johnson's—after he blasted Mariota off his feet and onto the ground.

"I don't know how you can call a guy down, or blow the whistle when he didn't hit the ground yet, especially on a sack," a frustrated Johnson said at his locker after the game. "It was a bad call."

The second instance came in the fourth quarter. Mariota had just thrown a touchdown pass that gave the Titans a 22-21 lead and they were going for two. Mariota took the snap, and Chiefs safety Daniel Sorenson blitzed from the edge. He corralled the Titans quarterback and literally threw him for a loss with the ball coming loose on a strip-sack.

Linebacker Frank Zombo picked it up and took it to the end zone for two points, which would have given the Chiefs the lead. But again the play was blown dead by the zebras. They ruled that Mariota's forward progress had been stopped.

In the aftermath, Chiefs coach Andy Reid wasn't happy with the officiating, but tried to bite his tongue as best he could.

"I don't really have anything good to say there or any comments on those guys," Reid said. "I'll just get fined. It's not worth it."

Triplette, who had not officiated a playoff game since January 2014, retired the day after the game.

Heavy hitter

Johnson made a name for himself as one of the league's hardest hitters and even his own teammates weren't sparred. At the 2014 Pro Bowl, Johnson delivered a helmet-to-helmet hit on Jamaal Charles, a close friend dating back to their days as Texas Longhorns.

In 2016 against Oakland, Johnson blew up a screen pass and put such a hard hit on running back Jalen Richard that the rookie just stayed down until the team's medical staff arrived to examine him. But one of Johnson's favorite hits came again against the Raiders in December 2017 at Arrowhead Stadium.

The Chiefs were reeling a bit having lost four in a row and six of seven. Leading by 19 midway through the fourth the Chiefs were finally in control, but the Raiders were driving. That is until Johnson sent Marshawn Lynch into orbit.

Lynch floated out of the backfield and had to look back over his shoulder and wait for Derek Carr's pass. Johnson, meanwhile, had nothing but air between him and Lynch. After they collided, Lynch landed 4 yards back, flat on his back, and the ball fell to his side incomplete.

"Whenever you get a chance to hit Beast Mode, and he's not looking, you take your shot," Johnson said. "He's a tough runner, one of the toughest runners to ever play against. So I took my shot."

Coaching career?

Johnson endured two gruesome injuries with the Chiefs. He ruptured the Achilles tendon in each leg, tearing his right one in the season opener in 2014 and the left one with three games remaining in 2016. Coming back from one Achilles tear is pretty remarkable, but coming back from two after age 30 is truly incredible.

"For coming back off of the two Achilles tendons, and playing at the level that he played at, that's tremendous," Reid said. "He comes out every day like he's 20 years old. I wish we all could do that. He loves life and loves every chance he has to be out here."

When he was on the sidelines, Johnson got to see football from a different perspective. While he always considered himself a coach on the field and off, he might actually be on the sidelines in the near future.

"Young guys will ask me questions," Johnson said. "They're picking my brain, seeing if I know my stuff. So I'm always on point with that. I enjoy it. Later in life I'd like to become some kind of a coach."

Johnson already has one coach firmly in his corner. After he signed with the Raiders as a free agent, Reid told him a spot on the Chiefs coaching staff awaits once his playing days are done.

"I'm going to be hard on him," Reid said. "But he can come back. Yeah, absolutely."

Johnson once said he hoped to play 15 years in the NFL, but he was released by the Raiders after six games last season and officially retired in May 2019 after signing a one-day contract with the Chiefs.

"I'm a Chief," Johnson said.

Justin Houston

Entering the final game of the 2014 season, Justin Houston needed 2.5 sacks to pass Derrick Thomas for the Chiefs' single-season sack record, set with 20 in 1990.

The Chiefs were already on the outside looking in at the playoff picture and needed three things to happen to make the postseason. They needed to beat the Chargers, and they needed the Ravens and Texans to lose.

The Chiefs did their part, knocking off the Chargers 19-7. But the Ravens and Texans rallied for second-half wins, and the Chiefs missed the playoffs for the first time in the Andy Reid era, finishing 9-7.

In an age of smartphones and social media, Chiefs players and coaches took preventative measures not to find out what was going on with the other two games of interest. But the other subplot to the day—Houston's shot at history—definitely had the attention of everyone in red. And, well, so did something else.

Entering play, the Chiefs had a rather dubious streak going. No Chiefs receiver had caught a touchdown pass all season. By game's end, the streak remained intact. The Chiefs came close on one play in the second quarter as Dwayne Bowe caught a pass from Alex Smith. But he fumbled the ball just short of the goal line and Travis Kelce recovered it in the end zone for the Chiefs' only touchdown of the day.

Later in the quarter, Houston recorded his first sack of the day. He got another near the end of the half, making him just half a sack shy of Thomas' mark. Early in the third quarter, Houston etched his name into the record books with a Thomas-style strip-sack of Philip Rivers. He also added another sack late in the fourth quarter, bringing his season total to 22—a half-sack short of Michael Strahan's NFL record set in 2001.

Even with a record-setting season under his belt, Houston has never really been one to boast about his own personal accolades.

"If I come out here and get 20 sacks in the game and we don't dominate as a whole, it doesn't matter what one person does," Houston said. "It's a matter of what we do."

The Incredible Houston

Under his helmet, Houston looks more like a warrior charging into battle than a linebacker. His legs are the size of tree trunks, but it's his arms that resemble the Incredible Hulk that really make him stand out.

One day in October 2003, when Houston was just a freshman at Statesboro High in Statesboro, Ga., those arms that weren't developed yet guided his two younger brothers out of their family's home which was engulfed in flames.

Houston never really had a father figure growing up, and he is the sixth oldest of 12 children. On this particular Saturday afternoon, he was in charge of the house, and he and his brothers went into their mother's room.

Young Tylen and Aaron were watching cartoons when Justin went to use the phone. The eerie silence of no dial tone told him something was wrong. He stepped out of the room and saw a door near the family's den ablaze with smoke pouring out all around it.

Frightened, he immediately ran outside and stopped when he thought he was safe. Then he realized his brothers were still inside. Immediately he ran back in. Amid smoke and fire and darkness, he found his brothers and guided them outside to safety.

The house was deemed a total loss, and the family lost everything. In the days and months that followed, the Statesboro community rallied around the family, providing food, clothing and shelter. The family eventually settled into another home outside of town, and Houston, who also played some point guard on the basketball team, become a football star and signed with Georgia.

His first year with the Bulldogs, Houston didn't go to class too often and redshirted. As a freshman, he didn't play much. As a sophomore, he was suspended two games for violating team rules. But as a junior, he showed promise, recording 11 sacks and becoming an All-American. At the NFL Combine in 2011, Houston bench pressed 225 pounds 30 times, which impressed everyone, but he tested positive for marijuana and his stock dropped far enough for the Chiefs to select him in the third round—70th overall.

As a rookie, Houston appeared in all 16 games and started 10, recording 5.5 sacks. In 2012, Houston earned his first of four straight Pro Bowls, recording 10 sacks that year, followed by 11 in 2013 and 22 in 2014.

Comparisons to Thomas were being made, but that wasn't really fair to Houston, who had 48.5 sacks in his first four seasons while Thomas had 58 sacks in his first four years. Though Houston made his name as an elite pass rusher, he could also hold his own in pass coverage and stop the run. In July 2015, the Chiefs rewarded him with a 6-year, $101 million contract with $53 million guaranteed. It was the largest contract in team history and the largest for a linebacker in NFL history at the time.

A slow down

Age can slow even the most physically gifted athletes. Add knee injuries to the mix and a career can take a drastic turn. That's essentially what happened to Houston, who was just 26 and entering his prime when the Chiefs gave him that mega deal.

Houston's troubles began when he hyperextended his knee in November 2015. He missed the last five weeks of the regular season, finishing with 7.5 sacks. He returned for the playoffs but was limited in both games.

During the offseason, he had his knee scoped. Doctors also found that his ACL had stopped working even though it wasn't torn. Houston played in only five games that season and recorded four sacks, three of which came in a thrilling Sunday night win at Denver.

He had a bounce-back season in 2017, playing in 15 games and recording 9.5 sacks. But he wasn't fully healthy all year.

"I didn't have all the strength in my leg," Houston said. "I was out there pretty much on one leg. No excuses. When you have surgery—the surgery that I had on my knee—it takes time. As much as you want to be ready it still takes time to get your pop back and get where you want to be."

'A part of the Chiefs family'

In 2018, Houston missed four games with a hamstring injury, but his knees held up, and he returned to form, recording nine sacks to go with a career-high five forced fumbles.

"When I come from the blind side it's easier to go for the ball than actually go for a big hit," Houston said. "Anytime I can cause that or get a shot on the ball that's what I go for."

Houston also had two sacks in the playoffs, but a salary cap hit of $21 million for the 2019 season was too much for the Chiefs, so they released him in a cost-cutting move, saving $14 million in cap space. He recorded 377 tackles, 96 tackles for loss and forced 14 fumbles as a Chief. Houston, who later signed with the Colts, finished his Chiefs career fourth on the team's all-time sack list with 78.5.

"Over the last eight seasons we've had the ability to watch Justin grow into a leader on and off the playing field," Chiefs chairman Clark Hunt said after Houston was released. "His passion helped him become one the most successful pass rushers in franchise history. We appreciate his contributions to our team and community, and he'll always be considered a part of the Chiefs family."

CHAPTER 13
DEFENSIVE BACKS

Johnny Robinson

Three broken ribs weren't going to keep Johnny Robinson out of Super Bowl IV. And time couldn't keep him out of the Pro Football Hall of Fame.

On Feb. 2, 2019, the day before the Super Bowl in Atlanta, Robinson, who starred at safety for the Texans/Chiefs, finally got the knock on his hotel door with news that he was one of eight members selected for the class of 2019.

Chosen by the veteran's committee, Robinson's selection comes about 40 years late as he was a big part of the Chiefs' two Super Bowl teams, an All-Pro six times and a Pro Bowler seven times.

"It's a thrill," Robinson, a former LSU standout, told the New Orleans Times Picayune. "There were times when I didn't think it would happen, but it did. To be able to join guys like Willie Lanier, Bobby Bell and Len Dawson, it's really special."

Robinson was first on the Hall of Fame ballot in 1977 and was a finalist six times in the 1980s. He will officially be inducted during a ceremony in August.

Robinson's selection coincided with Tony Gonzalez's as they will become the 13th and 14th players in Chiefs history to be enshrined in the Pro Football Hall of Fame. Robinson will be the sixth player on the Chiefs' Super Bowl championship defense to be enshrined, joining Lanier, Bell, Buck Buchanan, Emmitt Thomas and Curley Culp.

In Super Bowl IV, Robinson recovered a fumble in the first half and intercepted a pass in the fourth quarter.

Selected by the Lions with the third overall pick in the 1960 NFL Draft, Robinson instead signed with the Texans/Chiefs of the AFL, becoming one of the first players in franchise history. Robinson also is one of only a few players who played in all 10 seasons of the AFL's existence.

At LSU, Robinson played running back and helped lead the Tigers to the 1958 national championship. He also was a standout tennis player, winning an SEC singles title and a doubles title with his brother.

Robinson played his first two seasons at running back before Hank Stram moved him to safety where he became the team's quarterback on defense. During the next 10 years, Robinson picked off 57 passes, leading the AFL in INTs with 10 in 1966 and the NFL with 10 in 1970. He also was chosen to the AFL's all-time team.

Robinson retired following the 1971 season and later worked as a scout for Stram in New Orleans before becoming an assistant football coach and head tennis coach at Louisiana-Monroe. He also became an ordained minister and opened the Johnny Robinson Boys Home, a childcare facility in Monroe, La., in 1980.

Emmitt Thomas

Stepping away from the game is never easy, especially after 51 years. But at the conclusion of the 2018 season, Emmitt Thomas, the Chiefs Hall of Fame cornerback who coached the team's defensive backs the last nine seasons, officially called it a career.

"My journey started in Kansas City, and by the grace of God I am able to end my NFL career here as well," Thomas said. "I would like to thank the Hunt family and the Chiefs organization for all that they have done for me in my special days here in Kansas City. It has been a privilege to work alongside the great coaches that have come through this building.

"Having the opportunity to coach so many talented young men in my time as a coach has been one of my greatest gifts. I love Kansas City and this fan base and can't thank them enough for all the support they have given me in my time here as a player and a coach."

Thomas starred at cornerback for the Chiefs from 1966-78. He led the NFL in interceptions twice, made the Pro Bowl five times and had a key interception in the fourth quarter against the Vikings in Super Bowl IV.

Thomas was originally signed as an undrafted free agent out of Bishop College but ended his career with a franchise-record 58 interceptions. He was later elected to the NFL Hall of Fame in 2008.

"My last playing days were 1978, so I figured it was all over," Thomas said of his Hall of Fame chances. "I didn't think anyone else from the Chiefs in my era would possibly make it. After so long I just kind of gave up."

After his playing career ended, Thomas jumped right into coaching, starting with two seasons at Central Missouri State (1979-80). He then spent time with the St. Louis Cardinals (1981-85) before coaching receivers and defensive backs with the Redskins (1986-94) and earning two Super Bowl rings.

Thomas climbed the ladder and served as defensive coordinator with the Eagles (1995-98), Packers (1999) and Vikings (2000-01). From 2002-09 he was assistant head coach and defensive backs coach for the Falcons and was the team's interim coach for four games in 2007. In 2010, Thomas returned to the Chiefs and helped turn Eric Berry and Marcus Peters into Pro Bowlers.

"Over the course of a career that spans two leagues and most of the modern era of the NFL, Emmitt was a Hall of Fame player and one of the most respected coaches in the league," said Chiefs chairman Clark Hunt. "Emmitt will always be a part of our Chiefs family, and we wish him the best in retirement."

Lloyd Burruss

As the "quiet leader" of what would become possibly the best secondary in NFL history, one day Lloyd Burruss felt he had to speak up.

It was 1984, and a rookie cornerback named Kevin Ross was being unfairly called out for mistakes by the coaching staff. Burruss, who had started at strong safety since he was drafted in the third round out of Maryland in 1981, was the oldest of the group that included Deron Cherry, Albert Lewis and Ross so he had to approach the coaching staff.

"I remember standing up for Kevin in a meeting, telling the coaches that you're saying this player is doing something wrong, but it's not Kevin, it's someone else, because we had two players of the same stature and he was being mistaken for someone else, and Kevin kept telling them, 'That's not me.' And I had to tell a coach that," Burruss said with a laugh, while at the same time providing a glimpse into the difficulties the Chiefs faced in the 1980s before Marty Schottenheimer arrived.

Burruss, who played 11 seasons for the Chiefs, remains close friends with Ross to this day. Burruss grew up in the country in Charlottesville, Va., while Ross went to high school in New Jersey. That usually makes for good conversation.

"I'm an old country boy, and he's a city boy," Burruss said. "And he was always messing with me. When I call him, he does not address me as Lloyd. He calls me John-Boy, from 'The Waltons.' He always calls me that, he started that way back. That's what he calls me, John-Boy."

Burruss' father used to take him hunting as a kid, but his love for the outdoors didn't resonate with his four daughters.

Kansas City safety Lloyd Burruss (34) celebrates with cornerback Kevin Ross (31) after returning an interception for a touchdown against the San Diego Chargers on Oct. 19, 1986, at Arrowhead Stadium. Burruss had two pick-sixes that day and made the Pro Bowl that year. (Kenneth Spencer Research Library, University of Kansas Libraries)

"I get out to the country and I raised four daughters," Burruss said. "And my four daughters, man, they took off for the city."

Burruss, though, spent lots of time outdoors while he was living in Kansas City. Tuesday was the Chiefs' day off and he and other hunters on the team would go shoot.

"Kevin Ross made fun of that and said we couldn't hunt," Burruss said. "So one day when we all came in, all the hunters had T-bone steaks stuck inside their helmet raw."

Burruss also happened to live at the same apartment complex as Christian Okoye for a while.

"He always talked about how he ate goat, and I wanted to try it sometime because I never had it before," Burruss said. "And he fixed me some, and I went down to his room. And I got to say it was really rough, man. I got to say it was the roughest stuff I've ever ate. I tried it, I tried it. He laughed at me."

Burruss made the Pro Bowl in 1986 and finished his career with 628 tackles, 22 interceptions and seven fumble recoveries. He was inducted into the Chiefs Hall of Fame in 1999 and is regarded as one of the best tacklers of his era.

"Before they even started with the safety thing, it's something Kevin and I talked about," Burruss said. "Guys are not coming up and doing the things that we used to do. I loved it. I actually would get in trouble because I would want to make the tackle with a big hit and not take care of my responsibilities with the pass. So I had to learn to be disciplined that way. But I loved making tackles, loved making the big hit."

Since 1994 Burruss has been a personal trainer at ACAC Fitness in Charlottesville and he is enjoying retirement despite some leg pain from his football days.

"I have daughters and four grandkids, two boys and two girls," Burruss said. "God has blessed me. My mom and dad are still here and it's a blessing."

Deron Cherry

Originally signed by the Chiefs as a free-agent punter out of Rutgers in 1981, Deron Cherry made his mark as one of the top safeties in NFL history.

Moved to safety in training camp, Cherry was let go in the final round of roster cuts before the season opener. Cherry, though, was brought back in late September and spent his entire 11-year career with the Chiefs, recording 50 interceptions, third most in team history.

In 1981, the Chiefs drafted fellow safety Lloyd Burruss, and in 1983 and 1984 they drafted cornerbacks Albert Lewis and Kevin Ross, giving the Chiefs the best defensive backfield for the remainder of the decade.

Kansas City safety Deron Cherry had 50 career interceptions and was a force in stopping the run. (Kenneth Spencer Research Library, University of Kansas Libraries)

"You'd have to look deep into NFL history to find a group of players that played at a level compared to us during those years," Cherry said. "I think somebody was telling me this year that of all the defensive backfields, I think ours had played the most consecutive games together in NFL history. When you think about that, that's amazing. And to have all four of us be Pro Bowlers and All-Pros, that says a lot about how special that group was.

"I don't think we get the credit that we deserve for what we accomplished. We just happened to be in a situation where—and I try to tell people this all the time—but when you have so much turmoil and change that we had to be up against, and changing different systems every single year, we still had guys excelling and playing at such a high level."

In addition to being one of the game's best pass defenders, Cherry was a ferocious hitter. In a November 1990 game against the Raiders in Kansas City, Cherry returned to the lineup after suffering a serious knee injury the year before. He made his debut on the first play of the second quarter, the same time Bo Jackson went in the game.

Jackson took a handoff and burst through a hole for 7 yards. There to meet him was Cherry, who knocked Jackson backward and forced him to fumble, which the Chiefs recovered. It's a play Cherry remembers well, thanks in part to Chiefs cornerback Kevin Porter.

"That play has a lot of meaning for me and it's kind of a funny thing," Cherry said. "The interesting thing behind that was when I came into the locker room that morning Kevin Porter was in the training room and he looks at me and says, 'I had a dream about you last night.'

"It was kind of funny because he was lying on the table and he didn't have nothing but a towel on him. He was buck naked, and I told him, 'It wasn't what I think it is, is it?' and he just laughed and goes, 'No, I had a dream that your first play back, you hit the running back, and he fumbled, and we recovered the ball. And I said, 'OK, that's a good one. We'll see about that.'

"So first play of the second quarter, I just remember the Raiders lining up in I-formation. And I-formation for them was 100 percent run. So they hand the ball to Bo, and his first play and my first play back, he comes up, and it was just me and him between 90 yards of football field because if I missed a tackle or missed a play he's going the distance.

"So sure enough, he comes in and the ball pops out, and we recover. And the first person I saw was Kevin Porter. I went over to him to give him a high-five, and he kind of turned away from me like he had seen a ghost. He's leaving me hanging in front of 78,000 people and I'm going, 'Why'd you leave me hanging?'

"I get over to the sideline and I'm talking to him and he goes, 'Do you remember what I said to you in the locker room?' And it just hit me right there, the first play back, you're going to hit the ball carrier, and he was going to fumble, and we were going to recover, and that's exactly what happened."

Cherry played through injuries in 1991, including a bulging disc in his neck, and retired in July 1992. He was a six-time Pro Bowler and five-time All-Pro. Cherry led the team in tackles four times, recording more than 900 during his career. He also led the team in interceptions six times, was named to the Chiefs' all-time team in 1987—four years before he retired—and was named to the NFL's All-Decade team of the 1980s.

Cherry, though, played in just four playoff games, which has hurt his candidacy for the Pro Football Hall of Fame. He has never been a semifinalist but is optimistic he will someday be enshrined.

"I'm hopeful," he said. "I've had conversations. Rick Gosselin has called me a number of times and there have been other reporters who are on the Hall of Fame selection committee. I think I'm only one of three players in the entire history of the NFL who is not in the Hall of Fame that was on the All-Decade team of the '80s.

"If you look at our secondary as a whole, and as individuals, collectively there was no better secondary in the entire National Football League than what we had during the time we played. And from a numbers standpoint, there's not too many safeties in this league that have the same kind of numbers that I have, interceptions, tackles during the timeframe that I played and the number of games I played in. And I just think it's hard to put into words."

During his career, Cherry was one of the game's best humanitarians, winning the Byron "Buzzer" White Humanitarian award in 1988. Cherry remains just as active today. After he retired, he began a Budweiser distribution company and for a while was a minority owner of the Jacksonville Jaguars.

Cherry also has hosted the Deron Cherry Celebrity Golf Tournament for more than 25 years and helped found Kansas City University's Score 1 for Health program, which provides free health screenings and educational resources to children in the Kansas City area. In February, the school extended its reach to its campus in Joplin, Mo.

"This is the 25th anniversary year of the program and they decided to open it up and branch it out in Joplin for the College of Medicine," Cherry said. "I'm excited we can help those kids in that community."

Albert Lewis

49ers great Jerry Rice once said Albert Lewis was the toughest cornerback he ever played against. Lewis also happens to be one the best cornerbacks in NFL history.

Lewis played for the Chiefs from 1983-93 and was a key factor in the team's revival in the late '80s and early '90s under Marty Schottenheimer. Selected in the third round of the 1983 draft out of Grambling, Lewis was a backup his rookie season before earning a starting spot the following year.

Lewis once admitted he never watched game tape on his own in college but realized early in his NFL career that home study was must-see TV.

"When you first start looking at tape you realize you're really studying yourself more than the other team," Lewis recalled in *Hail to the Chiefs*. "You're trying to develop good habits. You are trying to see how you react to different situations rather than individual receivers."

In 1984 the Chiefs drafted Kevin Ross, and he and Lewis became the best cornerback duo in Chiefs history. NFL.com also ranked them as one of the top 10 cornerback tandems of all time. In 1985, Lewis may have had his best season. He recorded a career-high eight interceptions and 74 tackles. After that quarterbacks decided not to throw his way.

In 1987, he made the first of four straight Pro Bowls and was an All-Pro in 1989 and 1990. At 6-foot-2 and 196 pounds, Lewis could maul receivers at the line of scrimmage and run stride for stride with them down the sideline. He also wasn't afraid to lower his shoulder and help out against the run. Lewis had 555 tackles in his Kansas City career and was named to the Chiefs' all-time team in 1987.

In addition to being one of the top cornerbacks in the NFL, Albert Lewis (29) was an outstanding special-teams performer. In 11 seasons with the Chiefs, he blocked a franchise-record 10 punts and one field goal. Here he is celebrating with Deron Cherry (20) against the San Diego Chargers in 1986 at Arrowhead Stadium. (Kenneth Spencer Research Library, University of Kansas Libraries)

Lewis also was an outstanding special teams player. He blocked 10 punts as a Chief, including four in 1986 and 1990. Following the 1993 season, he became a free agent and played his last five seasons with the Raiders. Lewis had 42 interceptions in his career, 38 with the Chiefs.

Before the Chiefs' season finale in 1998, which was against the Raiders in Kansas City, Schottenheimer reflected on his former standout.

"He's the most gifted and best cornerback I have ever coached," Schottenheimer said. "I can still see him sitting on the airplane with that little recording video thing studying opponents as we're on the way to the game."

"For a guy like him, who's coached a lot of great players, that's a great compliment," Lewis said then. "He taught me how to play the position."

In 2005, Lewis served as Schottenheimer's defensive backs coach for one season in San Diego. In 2007, he was inducted into the Chiefs Hall of Fame. But like Deron Cherry he is not yet enshrined in Canton.

"I personally think Albert Lewis is as good a corner as I've seen play," Rick Gosselin said. "And you throw in the blocked kicks, he deserves to be discussed."

In July 2018, Lewis became ill and was hospitalized in a critical care unit in Shreveport, La. Ross, though, said his friend is improving.

"He's doing pretty well," Ross said. "He is recovering. I think he has good days and bad days, but most of them are good. But he's coming back to being himself again."

Kansas City Chiefs defensive back Kevin Ross was the final piece to the puzzle that formed the NFL's best secondary in the 1980s. Ross played 11 seasons for the Chiefs and was inducted into the team's Hall of Fame in 2011. Here he is warming up before a game against the Bills on Nov. 28, 1993, in Kansas City. (John Cordes/Icon Sportswire)

Kevin Ross

Though he'd rather be able to play, Kevin Ross is glad to be back on the sideline coaching the game he loves.

Ross, who starred at cornerback for the Chiefs from 1984-93 before returning for the 1997 season, joined Bruce Arians' staff as cornerbacks coach in Tampa Bay in January and said he can't wait for the 2019 season to begin.

"No question, I'm very excited," Ross said. "He's a great leader himself. He's a guy you can learn a lot from, and I've been soaking everything up. It's a great staff, great people."

Arians served as running backs coach for Marty Schottenheimer from 1989-92 and his relationship with Ross dates back further. Arians was head coach at Temple from 1983-88 and Ross played for him his senior season.

Ironically it was Ross' last year in the NFL when Schottenheimer told him he would make a great coach. Ross played in just five games that 1997 season after hurting his knee and going on injured reserve.

"Marty told me that I should investigate it and look into it," Ross said. "I did do it. I did it on the high school level. A friend of mine wanted to get into it so we drove down to Alabama together and tried to get into it, and I landed, and the rest is history."

Ross joined the NFL ranks as a defensive backs coach in 2004 with the Vikings and later served on Schottenheimer's staff in San Diego. After a two-year stint in Oakland, he joined Arians' staff with the Cardinals and coached there with him from 2013-17.

Drafted by the Chiefs in the seventh round of the 1984 draft, Ross became an immediate starter and recorded 827 tackles, 30 interceptions and made the Pro Bowl in 1989 and 1990 with the Chiefs. At 5-foot-9 and 185 pounds, he earned the nickname "Rock" for his solid and hard-hitting style of play, which Schottenheimer loved.

"I don't think I have been around anyone quite like Kevin," Schottenheimer said during Ross' playing days. "I've seen no evidence that he isn't ready to perform at any moment."

Though he didn't have the height of other defensive backs, Ross was a punishing hitter. One time at Arrowhead Stadium, he hit Seattle running back John L. Williams so hard it "even scared me a little bit," Ross said. And helping out in the run game is something Ross requires his defensive backs to do.

"It's all mindset," he said. "It's all training, that's all not wanting to let other people down. That's all that is right there. They keep howling about how much bigger the wide receivers and things are today, but that's false media. The running backs back then were much bigger than they are now. That's just a mindset and training, that's all that is."

Though Ross hopes to win a Super Bowl as a coach, he'd like to see Deron Cherry and Albert Lewis get the call to Canton just as much.

"There's a lot more passing today than there was then and still those guys got numbers that are better than most of the guys that's in there," Ross said. "So that's why I want to explain. You can't say durability because they played long enough. They've got the numbers. Why aren't they there?"

Eric Berry

It's Jan. 15, 2017, and a chilly night at Arrowhead Stadium. In a few minutes, the Chiefs will play the Pittsburgh Steelers in an AFC Divisional playoff game.

At the west end zone, Chiefs safety Eric Berry is down on one knee. Helmet off, his eyes gaze ahead, his every breath visible to the 75,000 fans in attendance, many of them wearing his No. 29 jersey.

As his teammates jog toward the tunnel to go to the locker room, Berry stays behind, still looking ahead, visualizing where he's come from, what he's gone through and what lies ahead.

"I do that all the time even in walkthroughs," Berry said. "Just going through everything. You can have a limit on physical reps but mental reps and visualizing and really painting that picture on how you want to play the game that plays a big role in what you actually do.

"I like to do that. I also like to appreciate the moment and take it all in and go from there."

It's a sight Chiefs fans have grown accustomed to seeing, but at the same time it's something they wish they'd seen a lot more of recently as injuries have pretty much wiped out Berry's last two seasons.

Berry has already overcome so much in his career, enduring pain that no one deserves—from injuries and fighting cancer. Somehow through it all Berry has kept a positive attitude and has become an inspiration to many with his courageous comeback story.

"I just keep on trucking, man," Berry said. "I don't know what life's going to throw at me and that's just period. You never know what's going to come your way. And however it comes to you, or whatever it is, you just roll with the punches and keep pressing forward."

Berry grew up just outside Atlanta in Fairburn, Ga. He attended Creekside High and played cornerback and quarterback and was rated by Rivals as the third-best prospect in the country. He attended Tennessee, where his father James played running back from 1978-81. The younger Berry became a standout safety, and the Chiefs selected him fifth overall in 2010.

Berry's first contract with the Chiefs was for six years and $60 million, with $34 million guaranteed. The deal made him the highest paid safety in NFL history and he hadn't yet played a down. Berry, however, went on to have an outstanding season. He didn't miss a snap and became the first Chiefs rookie since Derrick Thomas to make the Pro Bowl.

Chiefs safety Eric Berry pauses before the AFC Divisional playoff game against the Pittsburgh Steelers on Jan. 15, 2017, at Arrowhead Stadium. Berry played nine seasons for the Chiefs and served as an inspiration to many by overcoming cancer. (Scott Winters/Icon Sportswire)

Berry's second season in the NFL lasted two drives as he tore the ACL in his left knee in the opening quarter against the Bills in Week 1. He returned in 2012, starting all 16 games and earning another trip to the Pro Bowl.

In 2013, Andy Reid and Co. arrived in Kansas City, and Berry had arguably his best season to that point, recording 83 tackles while picking off three passes and retuning two of them for touchdowns. Berry earned another trip to the Pro Bowl and probably would have done so again in 2014 if he hadn't been in the hospital fighting for his life.

On Nov. 20, 2014, Berry told Chiefs doctors that he had some chest pains following their road loss to Oakland. A series of X-rays, blood tests and an MRI later revealed a mass on the right side of his chest, and Chiefs doctors suspected it was lymphoma. Berry immediately went to Emory University Hospital in Atlanta to seek treatment, and the diagnosis was confirmed to be Hodgkin's lymphoma.

At the time, Berry's doctors described the cancer as "very treatable and curable," but the news—like with any cancer diagnosis—put Berry's future as an NFL player somewhat in doubt.

Eight months later, however, he was back on the field with his teammates. The road to get there was unbelievably rough. Bi-weekly chemo treatments left him too weak to get out of bed some days, and on others he wasn't sure if he would live.

"Chemo is a whole different monster," Berry said. "You literally feel like you're dying every day. Really, when you're battling chemo, you're not battling chemo. You're battling yourself the whole time. It was me versus me.

"There were many times where I didn't know if I would wake up tomorrow. I'd just be up thinking, scared to go to sleep."

During treatment Berry's dad made his meals three times a day. His father loves to grill, and though chemo patients usually lose weight, Berry actually gained a pound. With that energy, Berry also worked out when he could as he prepared to come back for the 2015 season.

Berry chose to receive his chemo treatments through an IV rather than the standard method of using a PICC line, which leaves a catheter in the body between treatments. Most doctors and patients prefer the catheter because it's more convenient than dealing with needles and punctures each time. But that posed a problem for Berry as the catheter would restrict him from lifting any weight over 10 pounds.

Initially, because he was so weak, Berry's goal was to be able to do five pushups a day and progress from there. Eventually his workouts became so grueling that even he couldn't believe the strides he was making.

"There were times when I would work out and just be crying after the workout just because I couldn't believe I made it through," Berry said. "It was that hard."

In 2015, Berry played in all 16 games, made the Pro Bowl and won the NFL's Comeback Player of the Year award. It looked like his career was trending upward and his troubles were behind him. Turns out, there would be more difficulties ahead.

On Dec. 4, 2016, the Chiefs traveled to Atlanta to play the Falcons. In front of friends and family, Berry played the best game of his career. He had a pick-six in the second quarter and picked off a pass on a two-point conversion attempt late in the fourth and returned it for a score to give the Chiefs a thrilling 29-28 win.

While the Falcons went to the Super Bowl that season, the Chiefs lost to the Steelers in the playoffs despite not allowing a touchdown. Berry intercepted a pass in the end zone to thwart a Pittsburgh scoring opportunity in the second quarter, but it wasn't enough. After the game, Berry had a message for his teammates.

"Just look in the mirror and ask yourself if you did everything you could to win this game," Berry told them before they packed up for winter.

That offseason, Berry was unanimously named team MVP and got a new contract—six years for $78 million with $40 million guaranteed and a $20 million signing bonus, the richest ever for a defensive back.

Unfortunately, Berry's playing time decreased dramatically since signing on the dotted line. In the 2017 season opener at New England, Berry shut down Patriots tight end Rob Gronkowski but tore his Achilles late in the fourth quarter and missed the rest of the season.

Even though he couldn't play, Berry made a point to be around the team as much as possible. With the Chiefs mired in a four-game losing streak, he gave the team a passionate speech at midfield before a critical game against the Raiders.

With the All-Pro on the sideline, the defense held up, and the Chiefs won 25-15, taking a big step toward winning the AFC West.

"He's a legend in my eyes," said Chiefs defensive tackle Chris Jones. "Just the leadership qualities that he carries around this locker room. EB, he's a remarkable guy. Anytime he says something, you know it's legit, from the heart, and we can relate to it."

Linebacker Derrick Johnson echoed those sentiments.

"He's a guy that everybody looks up to," he said. "When he speaks, we listen."

Berry was back in action for the start of OTAs in May 2018, and the Chiefs believed he would be ready to go for Week 1 of the regular season. But more heel problems delayed his return. It's hard to believe, but Berry didn't practice and was listed as "day to day" on the team's injury report for more than 100 days.

Berry finally returned to action in December, playing in two games before returning to the sideline with pain in his foot/heel. He missed the playoff game against the Colts, but played every snap against the Patriots in the AFC championship game.

But Berry, 30, carried a cap hit of $16 million for the 2019 season and was released in March. He recorded 440 tackles, 14 interceptions and five sacks in nine seasons with the Chiefs.

"On behalf of my family and the entire Chiefs organization, I want to thank Eric for his many contributions to the Chiefs over the last nine seasons," Chiefs chairman Clark Hunt said. "Eric has been a tremendous leader for our football team and an inspiration to so many fans over the years, and we sincerely appreciate all that he has meant to the Chiefs. He will always be an important part of our Chiefs family, and we wish him nothing but the best in the future."

CHAPTER 14
SPECIAL TEAMS

Jan Stenerud

A ski jumping scholarship brought Jan Stenerud to the United States, but his foot carried him to the NFL Hall of Fame.

Stenerud was born on Nov. 26, 1942, in Festfund, Norway. The middle of three children, Stenerud took quickly to skiing—the most popular sport in the country back in those days. His father built him ski jumps at the family home, and Stenerud was mesmerized by the sport after watching the 1952 Winter Olympics in nearby Oslo.

By his late teens, Stenerud was competing at the Holmenkollbakken—Norway's most impressive slope—in front of more than 70,000 fans. At age 19, he received a skiing scholarship from Montana State and the chance at a free college education and getting to live in America was too good to pass up.

In 1964, Stenerud earned All-America honors as a skier and got his first taste of American football. To stay in shape, the ski team had to run the steps at Gatton Field. One day that fall, Stenerud, who played soccer as a kid, noticed Montana State football player Dale Jackson kicking field goals off the tee. Intrigued, Stenerud gave a long, close look.

"Hey Jan, you try it!" Jackson shouted.

Stenerud lined up and kicked a few with his toe straight on. Unfamiliar with the rules of the game, an idea popped in his head.

Chiefs kicker Jan Stenerud kicks a field goal against the Oakland Raiders on Nov. 23, 1969, at Municipal Stadium in Kansas City, Mo. Stenerud grew up in Norway and played for the Chiefs from 1967-79. In1991 he became the first pure kicker to be inducted into the Pro Football Hall of Fame. (Kenneth Spencer Research Library, University of Kansas Libraries)

"Can I kick with the side of my foot, like a corner kick in soccer?" Stenerud asked.

When told that was totally fine, Stenerud started blasting them through the uprights. Stenerud, however, didn't think much of it at the time so he went back to running stairs. A few weeks later, Stenerud was running the steps again when football coach Jim Sweeney spotted him.

"Hey skier, come down here!" he yelled. "I hear you can kick!"

Stenerud walked over, slipped on a pair of football shoes and connected from 70 yards away, with ease.

"Can you try one more time?" the coach asked.

Stenerud obliged, and connected three more times for good measure. Sweeney then put his arm around him.

"What are you doing tomorrow afternoon?" Sweeney asked.

Stenerud suited up for the team's final game of the season, but Sweeney elected not to have him take the field as he wanted Stenerud to just get acclimated to game day. In 1965, Stenerud made the team. Against Montana, he kicked a 59-yard field goal—the longest in the history of the game, both college and pro at the time.

Stenerud was an All-American that season and his 59-yarder got the attention of pro scouts and the Chiefs. At the end of the season, he got a telegram from Chiefs president Jack Steadman. It read:

"Congratulations! You have been drafted in the third round of the AFL Redshirt Draft. See you in Kansas City next year."

Stenerud still had one season of college eligibility remaining so he stayed in school and joined the Chiefs for the 1967 season. In preparation for his first training camp, he kicked field goals at Swope Park in Kansas City, with coach Hank Stram serving as his personal holder for about six weeks.

The sessions were invaluable to Stenerud, who got to know the coach he would grow to admire. The practices were even more beneficial for Stram, who later admitted that he "didn't know the first thing about a soccer-style kicker" and wanted to get a better perspective on Stenerud by studying his approach. Stram was so enthralled by the sidewinder that he even made charts on all of Stenerud's kicks.

"He pumped me up by telling me I was good," Stenerud said in Stram's autobiography *They're Playing My Game*. "He was great with nicknames, too. He called me 'Janski.' He was an outstanding coach."

Stenerud, who became an American citizen in 1976 and served in the National Guard during his days with the Chiefs, revolutionized the game with his deep kickoffs and lengthy field goals. In an era when the goalposts were stationed at the front of the end zone, with Stenerud the Chiefs were a threat to score every time they were near midfield.

Stenerud made his first kick with the Chiefs—a 54-yarder—and a couple seasons later he was kicking in the Super Bowl against the Vikings. He kicked three field goals in the first half as the Chiefs breezed to a 23-7 win.

Stenerud and the Chiefs returned to the playoffs in 1971, but a double-overtime loss to the Dolphins on Christmas Day at Municipal Stadium ended their hopes of returning to the Super Bowl. To many, the game is remembered for being the longest in NFL history at 82 minutes, 40 seconds. But for Stenerud, it's a memory he'd like to forget.

That 1971 Chiefs team may have been the most talented of the Stram era, but after missing three field goals against Miami, Stenerud blamed himself—and still does—for the loss.

"It's unbearable," he said in the locker room after the game. "It's totally unbearable."

On the first miss—a 29-yarder—Stenerud was actually supposed to be the ball carrier on a fake called by Stram. The Dolphins had a knack for overloading on one side on field goal attempts, leaving a hole on the other side. Stram thought the Chiefs could take advantage of this as Stenerud had exceptionally good speed for a kicker.

Bobby Bell—also the Chiefs long snapper—was supposed to snap the ball directly to Stenerud, who was supposed to run around the right side and pick up the first down or possibly take it to the end zone.

Stenerud was just as surprised as holder Len Dawson when the ball was snapped directly to the Hall of Fame quarterback and not him. When Bell looked back between his legs before the snap, he thought Stenerud didn't look ready to run the fake.

Bell figured Stenerud didn't hear the audible in the huddle so he threw it to Dawson instead. With the timing of the fake disrupted, Dawson could only say one thing.

"Kick it!" he yelled.

Stenerud, already halfway in motion to run, had to adjust on the fly and missed the kick by just a few inches to the right. Had the fake been run successfully, Stenerud likely would have scored a touchdown.

The second miss came on a 31-yarder late in the fourth quarter. This time the snap and hold were good, and when the ball left Stenerud's foot he thought he had made it. But the ball sailed just past the right upright, forcing overtime with the scored tied at 24.

In the fifth quarter, Stenerud had a 42-yard attempt blocked, and midway through the sixth quarter, Miami kicker Garo Yepremian connected on a 37-yarder to end the Chiefs season. The pain of losing was so great that Stenerud thought about walking away from the game altogether, but Stram convinced him to keep kicking. And 20 years later, Stenerud became the first pure kicker to be enshrined in the Hall of Fame.

Stenerud was the last of the Super Chiefs to wear the uniform. That ended in August 1980 when Marv Leavy opted to go with the younger Nick Lowery, who went on to have quite a career himself. In his 13 seasons with the Chiefs, Stenerud led the NFL in field goals made three times and was a five-time Pro Bowler.

His field goal percentage with the Chiefs was just 64 percent but that was about the league average at the time. Back then there weren't many dome stadiums, making weather and field conditions a formidable foe. Teams also didn't practice special teams on a regular basis like they do now.

After his release, Stenerud played six more seasons in the NFL—four with Green Bay and two with Minnesota. After living in Colorado, he and his wife moved back to Kansas City a few years ago.

Nick Lowery

The Pro Bowl has sort of lost its luster over the years, but for Nick Lowery, the All-Star exhibition made for some of the best memories of his life.

Lowery, the Chiefs' star kicker from 1981-93, was selected to the Pro Bowl for the 1982, 1990 and 1992 seasons. All three times, Lowery kicked the game-winning field goal. He remembers fondly getting hugs from Derrick Thomas and Junior Seau after making a 33-yard kick in February 1993 to give the AFC a 23-20 overtime win.

The hugs from Thomas and Seau bookend his Pro Bowl career nicely, considering his first one ended the same way with a bit of a twist, courtesy of Steelers Hall of Fame linebacker Jack Lambert.

"The first one, back then, it was $10,000 for the winner and $5,000 for the loser," Lowery said. "And Jack Lambert gave me this big toothy grin and said, 'Rookie,' he called me rookie because I looked so young. He said, 'Rookie, you make this kick, we make $10,000 if you make it, and $5,000 if we lose it. Make it or I'll rip your fucking head off! So then he gave me this big smile.

"He was the left wing on the field goal team, and the left wing, you have to lean to your right against the line so nobody can jump through that pocket because you're a half-step behind. And then you spin out to your left so the guy can't come around the corner to block it, and by doing that you had to spin. So he spins and sees the ball going through, runs over and almost breaks my ribs hugging me, which is a lot better than ripping my head off."

From DC to KC

Lowery's path to the Pro Bowl was a circuitous one. He kicked in college at Dartmouth and was a two-time All-Ivy league selection. In 1978, he appeared in two games with the Patriots but was cut. In 1978 and 1979 he was released or rejected 11 times by eight different teams.

To help pay the bills, Lowery, who majored in government, got a job working as a legislative aide for Sen. John Chafee of Rhode Island. With a good job, Lowery's dreams of a career in the NFL were put on the backburner.

"I had pretty much given up," Lowery said. "I had gotten a job working for the Science and Transportation Committee and decided that here I got a nice job in the Senate, and when you work for a committee, you're not fired when your senator loses his or her job. So it was a great job working on aviation deregulation and aviation safety and the Olympic boycott and all sorts of different things."

But on the Saturday of the NFL Wild Card games in 1980, Lowery got a call from Chiefs general manager Jim Schaaf, who had just undergone back surgery.

"I already had pretty much rejected two contract offers from the Cleveland Browns and Baltimore Colts," Lowery recalled. "I tried out with the Colts twice, and here I had a contract offer from them so I told Jim Schaaf, 'Thank you so much, but I got a great job now so maybe some other time.' And the second I hung up on him I was like, 'Oh, shit! What did I just do?'"

Lowery placed a call to his old high school coach Dick Johnson, who urged him to call Schaaf back. Lowery didn't have his number—that was back before cellphones—so he dialed information in Kansas City and eventually was directed to the hospital Schaaf was staying at.

"After I hung up with this stranger, I found him in this hospital room in his hospital bed, and we talked for an hour," Lowery said. "They flew me out early the next week, I think on a Tuesday, and I remember it snowed about a foot.

Kansas City kicker Nick Lowery celebrates after making a field goal against the Seattle Seahawks on Nov. 11, 1990, at Arrowhead Stadium. Lowery played 14 seasons with the Chiefs and is the team's all-time leading scorer with 1,466 points. (Kenneth Spencer Research Library, University of Kansas Libraries)

"They drove me in for a physical, and I was up in the office there with Jim Schaaf. He talked about how Marv Levy had been the first special teams coach for George Allen back in the day and what happened was they offered me a $2,500 bonus, which today would be considered a joke.

"But they said they would bring me in in May. And before I had just come to training camp for the Bengals, Redskins and for the New York Jets, I had never been there in May. And I thought that would really help me get ready and I owe it to myself to try one more time.

"So I decided to give up that really awesome job that's very, very hard to get in the Senate, one that's almost as hard to get as an NFL placekicker's job, and try one more time. And when I talk to kids today I talk about how those two years of being cut made me so much better. And it's all about timing, and I was ready. I was so much more ready, mentally tougher."

Nick the Kick

Lowery credits much of his success in the NFL to the early teachings of Johnson, who had never kicked himself but had knowledge that shaped Lowery's career.

"He was the first one to say you've got to learn intentionally—and that's one of my favorite words—to manage your mental state and learn to relax and get in that right place because as a kicker you're really like Billy the Kid," Lowery said. "You've got to come out and you've got one shot. You either win or you lose, there's nothing in between.

"And that really helped me and because I think of that, kicking the game-winning field goal in really sloppy weather in the rain, literally the last second of my high school career to beat our rival Landon, that was just a hint."

Lowery trained all April to be ready for his shot with the Chiefs. To make the squad, he knew he had to outkick Jan Stenerud, an iconic figure from the

Super Bowl IV team, every single day in practice. In August, the Chiefs made their choice and kept Lowery and released Stenerud.

Lowery's first field goal was from 50 yards away against Seattle in Week 2 at Arrowhead.

"You know, back in 1980, a 50-yarder today is a joke for a lot of kickers because the ball is so much easier to kick," Lowery said. "Granted, they are good kickers, but the ball is a lot easier to kick, and Stenerud's just amazed that no one has talked about that. But the ball is broken in now and before it wasn't."

Lowery drilled that 50-yard attempt in the third quarter and later in the fourth quarter he kicked a 57-yarder, breaking Stenerud's record for the longest field goal in franchise history. It also marked the first time in NFL history that a kicker made two 50-yarders in a game.

For the rest of the decade, Lowery was in a class by himself. And many believe he still is. In a 2015 study, Chase Stuart of FootballPerspective.com makes a compelling argument that Lowery is the greatest kicker of all time.

In the 1980s, Lowery had the most field goals (225) and was the most accurate kicker of the decade (77.6 percent). He also led all kickers in kicking percentage in the 1990s at 84 percent.

Following the 1993 season, Lowery was released by the Chiefs in a cost-cutting move. The Chiefs signed Linn Elliott, and Lowery played his final three seasons with the Jets. When Lowery retired he had the most field goals in NFL history with 383, his 80-percent accuracy rate was the best in history, and he also had the most 50-yarders in history with 22.

Factoring in distance and era in which he played, Stuart says Lowery's expected field goal percentage was just 70.5 percent and the fact that he made 80 percent was "remarkable." Lowery also made 15 game-winning kicks in his career and that's not all.

"I had about 40 which were the deciding points in the fourth quarter, which is pretty important," Lowery said. "And when Marty was my coach, at one point I was 38 for 40 in the fourth quarter."

While many consider Lowery the best kicker of his era, he is not in the Pro Football Hall of Fame yet. To date, there are only two kickers enshrined in Canton—Stenerud and Morten Anderson.

Anderson, who was enshrined in 2017, played 25 years in the NFL, more than 20 of those in a dome. Lowery, meanwhile, spent his career kicking outdoors and somehow made 85 percent of his kicks at Arrowhead Stadium.

"If I would have been a combination of indoors and outdoors I would have been so far ahead of everybody else," Lowery said.

Lowery, who was inducted into the Chiefs Hall of Fame in 2009 and is the team's all-time leading scorer with 1,466 points, also converted 562 of 568 PATs, an incredible 98.9 percent.

"I figured out something really important as I got later into my career, which is true and it's been proven in chemistry and psychology," Lowery said. "When you are self-conscious, the body turns on the large muscle groups. When you are in the flow and simply being yourself and trusting your natural God-given talent—whether it's the swing of hitting a tennis racquet, or hitting a baseball or golf club or swinging with your leg or the swing of your pivot as you play basketball or running out your stride—all of those things are natural and they are infinitesimally finite and subtle.

"So you've got find a way to just relax and do it and not worry about missing. So what I would say as I was approaching the ball my last few years in the league, which made me even more successful in the big kicks, was left foot, explode.

"Left foot was left foot at the target, right at the target. That's when I knew I had perfect alignment so when my foot would hit the ball my hips would be exactly square to the target, and then explode. And that word worked for me, which was attack it.

"Not trying to kill it, but by attacking it you're still aggressive. But you're just releasing it. So when the ball has that natural power behind it, it fights the wind better. The ball will naturally slow down right at the beginning. And if you are a powerful kicker in the NFL you start losing speed at about 40 yards and the average kicker you start losing speed at 35 yards.

"So I was closer to 40, but if I tried to be too precise, and tried to just get it perfect, then it would start slowing down at 30 yards. So then in a big game with a big wind it would push it not just for the final 10 yards but for the final 20 yards, and I love that because wind can represent adversity. In other words, the more you attack, and as Frank Ganz would say, 'Fortune favors the bold.' And bold does not mean stupid, but it does mean aggressive. And if you think about Joe Montana and Tom Brady and Patrick Mahomes, they aren't tentative."

Nick Lowery waves to the crowd as he walks off the field after kicking the game-winning field goal in overtime to give the Chiefs a 27-24 win in the playoffs against the Pittsburgh Steelers on Jan. 8, 1994, at Arrowhead Stadium. (Kenneth Spencer Research Library, University of Kansas Libraries)

'I'm really blessed'

During his playing career, Lowery's agent was Leigh Steinberg. And Steinberg, along with Chris Cabott, represents Mahomes. Every year at the Super Bowl, Steinberg throws a party for his clients. So the day before Super Bowl LIII in Atlanta, Lowery, who received the 2019 Steinberg-DeNicola Humanitarian award for community service, bumped into Mahomes.

The two took selfies together, and Mahomes was on stage with Lowery when he received his award. At one point, Lowery pulled him aside to talk in private.

"I said to him backstage, 'Let's get ourselves like three Super Bowl rings,'" Lowery said. "And he goes, 'Why stop there?' I like that response."

Since retiring, Lowery has lived in Arizona for more than 20 years. He had prostate cancer last fall, but said he is "doing great" and in February he received the Pillar of Excellence award from the American Cancer Society.

Lowery enjoys public speaking and is working with Kannalife Sciences to create an "intercellular helmet" that would make the game safer and reduce concussions, a cause dear to him as he has lost friends, including Seau and former teammate Mike Webster, to CTE.

"That's what binds us all, and the Super Bowl, it's those relationships," Lowery said. "It's not fox-hole Army buddies, but it's close. You've bled together, you've trained together, you've gone through humiliating defeats and incredible victories.

"You've worked your tails off together, you've dealt with incredible pressure in a very public way and in a lot of private moments together. You travel together, and it's just something that is so beautiful and unique. I'm really blessed, and with all the things I'm working with to reduce concussions to honor people like Mike Webster, my teammate for two years, it still is the best game ever. And it's the best thing that ever happened to me."

Dante Hall

He cuts left, then right, then left again. Now with nowhere to go Dante Hall runs backward toward his own end zone.

Punt returners are not supposed to field a ball behind their own 10 yard line, yet there was Hall just a few yards from the goal line with a herd of Broncos surrounding him on a sunny October day in 2002 at Arrowhead Stadium.

At that moment, Hall was on the brink of making history. He had already returned a kick for a touchdown in his previous three games and was going for a record fourth straight when he ran left and found a seam with a row of Chiefs directly in front of him.

The Chiefs were trailing 23-17 midway through the fourth quarter, but 93 yards later Hall had outrun everybody to the end zone for a touchdown, propelling the Chiefs to a 24-23 victory with his fourth touchdown return in as many weeks and his seventh in 10 games dating back to the 2001 season.

Initially, when Hall started running backward, he thought he might get tackled for a safety and thus give the game to the Broncos.

"I thought, 'Oh, I've got to get out of this jam,'" Hall told reporters after the game. "The first part of that return was not smart. I caught it maybe on the 8, then I retreated back to the 5, then the 2. I got dumber and dumber."

On the sideline, Chiefs coach Dick Vermeil watched in dismay as Hall ran backward, then he cheered as Hall broke free.

"I was beside myself I was so excited for him," Vermeil said. "I said to myself, 'Oh Dante, don't go backward.'"

Hall electrified the Chiefs as a return specialist from 2000-06, earning the nicknames "X-Factor" and the "Human Joystick" for his video-game like ability while returning kicks and punts, catching passes or taking a reverse as a slot receiver.

As a return man, Hall made the Pro Bowl in 2002 and 2003 and was an All-Pro in 2003. Hall is the Chiefs' all-time leader in returns (360), kickoff return yards (8,644) and kick return touchdowns (6). He's also the franchise leader in punt return touchdowns with five.

Hall was the Chiefs' fifth-round pick in 2000, selecting him as a running back out of Texas A&M. At 5-foot-8 and 187 pounds, he wasn't really built for the position and he didn't have a single carry or reception his first two years in the league.

In 2001, Hall played for the Scottish Claymores in NFL Europe and learned to play slot receiver. From 2002-06, he became a triple threat in the Chiefs' record-breaking offense, catching 145 passes for 1,615 yards and scoring nine touchdowns to go with 242 yards rushing.

Hall was traded to St. Louis after the 2006 season and played his final two years there. His 12,397 career return yards rank sixth in NFL history and he was named to the NFL's All-Decade team of the 2000s as a returner.

Dustin Colquitt

Finishing what you start is an admirable feat. While the task at hand can sometime take years to accomplish, the end result might be worth the wait.

Chiefs punter Dustin Colquitt is hoping for that. He has spent 14 seasons in a Chiefs uniform and is the team's all-time leading punter. While Colquitt has been to the Pro Bowl twice, he has never played in the Super Bowl—at least not yet.

However, Colquitt believes if he plays his cards right, that could happen in the very near future. And even if it does, he has no plans to stop kicking anytime soon.

A lock for the Chiefs Hall of Fame, Colquitt could also land in the Pro Football Hall of Fame someday. He is a funny, charismatic and caring person who spends much of his time bringing smiles to others. And to him, that's what's most important.

Ring of fire

Colquitt's father, Craig, won Super Bowl rings as a punter with the Pittsburgh Steelers in 1978 and 1979. His brother, Britton, also won a Super Bowl ring as the punter for the Broncos in 2015.

So when the three of them get together, do Craig and Britton constantly remind Colquitt that he does not have a ring?

"Always," Colquitt said. "It's definitely not in a good-natured way. It's just not. That's definitely another one of the reasons why I wanted to be back and have a chance to do it here in Kansas City."

Kansas City Chiefs punter Dustin Colquitt points to the sky after a punt against the Pittsburgh Steelers on Sept. 16, 2018, at Heinz Field. Colquitt is the team's all-time leading punter and ranks third in NFL history with 441 punts downed inside the 20. (Mark Alberti/Icon Sportswire)

After the 2017 season, Colquitt was a free agent and could have signed elsewhere. But after a talk with his father, he knew there was only one place he wanted to be. So he signed a three-year deal to remain with the Chiefs.

"He was just adamant about me staying here and finishing the task," Colquitt said of his father. "He's always been about finishing contracts, and make sure they sign up for a winner, and to be that, and embrace community. All the things that Kansas City preaches anyway, he wanted me to finish it out here."

After a standout career at Tennessee, the Chiefs drafted Colquitt in the third round in 2005. That year, the Chiefs also selected Derrick Johnson in the first round.

"When me and Derrick came in here, we all got cards, which I still have," Colquitt said. "It has a picture of the Lombardi Trophy saying, 'The main thing is the main thing.' And I've kept that card."

The Chiefs in 2019 might be closer to reaching that goal than at any point in the last 50 years, and that has Colquitt excited.

"We've got to complete that as a team. We have everything in this room. As Coach Reid and (Brett) Veach say, they're just trying to build on that and make us more competitive. So that's the biggest thing they've brought to the table is they're continuing to pump talent in, get the best guys out there available, and just try to win a championship.

"They say that behind closed doors, that's what their goals are. They get up every day, and they're sitting around an oval table and saying, 'How do we win a championship here?' That's what the Hunt family wants, and that's what this city needs."

Chiefs fans would also like to see Colquitt keep playing deep into the future. And with Patrick Mahomes at quarterback, they might get their wish. Colquitt hopes to play enough to one day pass Royals icon George Brett as the longest-tenured player the city has ever had.

Brett played for the Royals from 1973-93 so Colquitt has some catching up to do if he is going to pass his friend.

"I've just been in too many close quarters with him claiming the longest longevity. I'm going to try to play longer than he did here," Colquitt said, somewhat jokingly. "I feel good. I feel good every year. My body still feels like I can play, seven, eight, nine years.

"I still feel like Adam Vinatieri. I try to follow what Jeff Feagles did. He started swimming and really taking care of his knees and body and he was able to make a Pro Bowl in year 21. So I feel like if I'm eating good, and hanging out with these young guys, I'm going to be feeling younger already. I already act really young over there at the facility anyway. I'm sure you've heard stories."

High praise

Punters don't get much limelight, but they are vitally important to the success of a football team. Colquitt's career average of 44.9 yards per punt is better than Hall of Famer Ray Guy's and Colquitt ranks third in NFL history with 441 punts inside the 20.

"He's been doing it his whole career, well before I got here," said Chiefs special teams coach Dave Toub. "He has a knack for having a touch with his leg and knowing exactly where to put it, playing the wind, understanding who the gunners are, who the returner is. And he just has a great feel for it."

Playing in ideal conditions is always best for kickers and punters, but that's not going to happen playing in the Midwest. Colquitt, however, likes punting in the wind, partly because it presents an opportunity to improve.

"When you are going into the wind, you want to have a level drop," he said. "You don't want the nose to drop or come up. The biggest thing you don't want is the nose to fall because then you have a line-drive punt. That's what Tyreek (Hill) is going to get a lot. He is going to get directional kicks, kicks trying to get out of bounds, lot of rugby stuff.

"It is good for him to get, it is good for me to get. Whenever we have weather like that it changes our direction. It's just as crucial for me because the ball acts differently, too, when it is wet on that turf kicking up. Wind gives you a chance to get better because you are working on different stuff that could arise during the year."

Call to serve

Throughout his time in Kansas City, Colquitt has been active in many charities, including TeamSmile, Play 60, Athletes in Action, and the Fellowship of Christian Athletes. In 2018, he was the Chiefs nominee for the Walter Payton Man of the Year award.

"As a player, Dustin has been among the best at his position for the entirety of his career," said Chiefs chairman Clark Hunt. "As a teammate, his loyalty to the Chiefs organization is unparalleled, and his character and charisma make him an invaluable leader to our team. None of those attributes, however, compare to Dustin's commitment to the Kansas City community."

Colquitt also was the team's nominee in 2009.

"Having the Chiefs blessing as the Walter Payton NFL Man of the Year nominee humbles my heart," Colquitt said. "This organization and city have embraced me from the first time I stepped through the doors.

"There is a huge calling to serve others in this life, and you can do that with love, time, talents and effort, and Walter Payton embodied that through an incredible ability to reach people and communities with his soul and his passions."

Harrison Butker has been right on target since becoming a member of the Chiefs. As a rookie in 2017 he set the franchise record for field goals in a season with 38. (Scott Winters/Icon Sportswire)

Harrison Butker

Harrison Butker had butterflies as he stepped onto the field to attempt a game-winning 43-yard field goal in his NFL debut on Oct. 2, 2017.

He had just arrived in Kansas City a few days earlier, and many people on the team only knew him by the No. 7 on his jersey. The Chiefs and Redskins were tied at 20 with less than 10 seconds to play when Butker walked onto the field that windy Monday night at Arrowhead Stadium.

Hours earlier when the game began, Butker was kicking with a 14 mph wind from the south/southeast. The first attempt of his NFL career was a 46-yarder on the west side of the field that sailed wide left to end the first half. About 90 minutes later, Butker found himself looking into the same west end zone this time with the game on the line.

As he eyed the goalpost in front of him, he had some insight, courtesy of his missed field goal before halftime.

"I think everything happens for a reason," Butker said. "I missed that kick, came back. I was more experienced going that way, more experienced with the wind."

The Redskins called timeout, trying to ice the rookie kicker who was signed off Carolina's practice squad. It didn't matter. On his second attempt into the end zone where he missed his first kick in the pros, Butker hammered the ball through the uprights for the game-winner—although on the ensuing kickoff Justin Houston returned a fumble for a touchdown to make the final score 29-20 Chiefs.

"The first kick of the night was down the middle, and I missed it left," Butker said. "Looking back now it was probably a good thing I missed. I was used to the wind. I knew the ball was going to move and that allowed me to aim right down the middle on the second kick."

Prior to that Butker's only other game-winner came in 2014 when he was at Georgia Tech. That kick was only 26 yards so this one was indeed extra special. After he made it, Butker clenched his fists and ran, screaming in jubilation as he was mobbed by teammates.

"That was my first long field goal for a game-winner," Butker said. "They froze me, and then I was able to kick the ball. And I think that was able to help me, to get a practice kick.

"I aimed for the middle with the wind, and it went down the middle. I think it went down the middle. I don't know. I just turned around and started running."

In two seasons with the Chiefs, Butker has already set team records and established himself as one of the premier kickers in the NFL.

'Lucky' seven

Butker grew up in Decatur, Ga., and played tuba in the high school band. As a kid, his first love was soccer. His goal was to play in the MLS but his focus changed his sophomore year when the varsity football coach asked him to be the team's kicker.

After his junior season, several schools began recruiting him, and he eventually picked Georgia Tech. As a senior, he was a team captain and finished his career as the school's all-time leading scorer. The Chiefs were high on Butker in the draft, but the Panthers selected him in the seventh round with the 233rd overall pick.

The Panthers kept Butker on their 53-man roster for the first two weeks of the 2017 season and placed him on the practice squad for a week. But after an injury to Cairo Santos in Week 3, the Chiefs needed a kicker and Butker was the one they wanted.

"Every year we rank the kickers, no matter if we're looking for a guy or not, kickers, punters, snappers and then position guys, too," said Chiefs special teams coordinator Dave Toub. "He was our No. 1 kicker coming out. When Cairo got hurt, we just went back to our list, and he was available, and we kind of got lucky that he was still on the practice squad, and we were able to pick him up."

At 6-foot-4 and 205 pounds, Butker definitely has a strong leg. In 2017, he was 4 of 5 from 50 yards or more and in 2018 he kicked a career long of 54. Butker, though, says his range extends to 60 yards.

"I think most kickers can do that," he said. "To be in the NFL, you kind of have to be able to do that. But wherever they put me, I feel like I'm comfortable. As long as it's 60 and in I don't think I'm changing anything with my form, just kick it smooth."

After missing his first kick as a rookie, he made his next 23 to set a team record for consecutive field goals made. In 2017 he connected on 38 of 42 field goals and shattered the club record for field goals made in a season despite not being on the roster the first three games of the year.

In 2018, Butker kicked made 24 of 27 field goals as his opportunities were much fewer with Patrick Mahomes at quarterback. Since becoming a Chief, Butker has learned how difficult kicking in the Midwest can be. Rain, snow and wind are just some of the elements he has to perform in. Ironically, he said kicking in practice can be more difficult than kicking under the bright lights.

"Our practices are a lot windier than the games," he said. "I don't know why that is. Usually stadiums generate more wind than what you experience at practice. But at practice there's been a ton of wind, and if I can do well in practice, when I get to the game, it's nothing. You've to account for it, but it's not a huge deal."

'Buttkicker.com'

Chiefs coach Andy Reid is pretty good at being even keeled. He's also pretty good with one-liners. After Butker made his game-winning kick against the Redskins, Reid was asked if he had a nickname for the kicker he had only known a few days.

"Buttkicker.com," Reid said to the amusement of the media at his postgame press conference.

At that time, there was no actual webpage with that address. But soon after, Butker started his own website at buttkicker7.com. Before he even got to the Chiefs, Butker already was quite popular on social media thanks to his @buttkicker Twitter handle.

"It came from a trainer at Georgia Tech my freshman year," Butker said of his famous nickname. "He just said 'butt kicker' and I was like, 'Oh, that's pretty interesting, and it's unique.' People say a lot of stuff with my last name being Butker, and I kind of made it a funny thing to now be 'butt kicker.' I just went with it."

Chiefs fans are glad he did, and so is Butker, who agreed to a five-year contract extension in June worth $20.3 million, making him the NFL's highest-paid kicker.

"It's a lot of fun," Butker said. "The locker room is a bunch of really good guys. They're all very supportive of me and they're very encouraging. I've loved every moment. The coaches are great, they've been very encouraging as well. So I really like it here. I feel very comfortable."

CHAPTER 15
LEGENDS IN THE MAKING

The Class of 2019

Every offseason in the NFL brings change. Players come and go, coaching staffs and schemes change. The Chiefs have undergone several changes since that loss to the Patriots in the AFC championship game.

On the coaching side, Steve Spagnuolo is now defensive coordinator and Bob Sutton is not. The Chiefs also overhauled the staff on that side of the ball and are switching to a 4-3 scheme. With that in mind, Dee Ford was traded to the 49ers, and Justin Houston and Eric Berry were not brought back.

Whether through free agency, trades or the draft, the arrival of new players often brings a level of hope and excitement that they will become the next in a long line of Chiefs greats. Though the 2019 offseason was rather tumultuous, the Chiefs may have solidified several positions for years to come.

They signed coveted free agent safety Tyrann Mathieu, defensive ends Alex Okafor and Emmanuel Ogbah and running back Carlos Hyde. In Mathieu, the former Pro Bowler and All-Pro whose nickname is "Honey Badger," the Chiefs believe they have a versatile player who can be a leader on and off the field.

"Obviously when you have a team like we do, you're going to put a lot of points on the board so teams are going to have to throw to get back in the game," Chiefs general manager Brett Veach said. "And when you have a guy as talented as Ty, he can play in the deep end, he can play down low, he can play in the slot, he's a tremendous blitzer, he's a versatile piece to the puzzle, and then you factor in the person and the character what he brings intangibly, that's why we coveted him and made a point to make sure he was with the Chiefs this season."

Mathieu, who spent five seasons with the Cardinals and one with the Texans, said signing with the Chiefs was an easy decision.

"My biggest job is to come here, be a leader and try to make plays on and off the football field and put my hand in the pot and help us win some games," Mathieu said. "I wanted to come to a team that obviously had great talent, great core players, and their core players are still young, closer to my age. So I think that had a lot to do with the decision as well. And any time you can play for an organization with a great history, obviously a young quarterback that's really going to take over this league by storm, really, it was a no-brainer for me and my family."

A few weeks after signing Mathieu, the Chiefs traded their first-round pick to Seattle for defensive end Frank Clark. In four seasons with the Seahawks, Clark had 35 sacks and also helped stop the run.

"This was our plan all along," Veach said. "This was our target. As you guys know, I'm rather persistent and when we find someone we like, we find a way to get him."

In the second round of the draft, the Chiefs moved up to take Georgia wide receiver Mecole Hardman, maybe the fastest player in the draft.

"We were looking at the board and, again, you're never going to pass up speed," Veach said. "When you looked at the wideouts there was still a lot of good wideouts left, but none that ran 4.27."

The Chiefs also ranked Hardman as the top kick and punt returner in the draft.

"We like his speed," Chiefs coach Andy Reid said. "But he's more than that. He can play inside, he can play outside, he did both at Georgia. And he's a phenomenal returner, arguably the best returner in the draft, and we look forward to adding him to our wide receiving corps. This is somebody Brett had his eye on from the get-go. It doesn't have anything to do with things going on now (with Tyreek Hill). It's a player that he's felt very good about."

With their second pick in the second round, the Chiefs selected Virginia safety Juan Thornhill, who had 13 career interceptions for the Cavaliers. It's possible Thornhill could even start Week 1 at Jacksonville.

"He gives you a lot of flexibility," Reid said. "He can play safety, he can play nickel, can play either safety, in the box or on the back end or corner."

In the third round, the Chiefs picked Western Illinois defensive lineman Khalen Saunders, an athletic 324-pounder who does backflips, and they closed out the draft by selecting South Carolina defensive back Rashad Fenton, Utah State running back Darwin Thompson and Illinois offensive lineman Nick Allegretti.

After drafting Fenton in the sixth round, Veach immediately began calling teams to try and trade up to draft Thompson but a deal couldn't be reached. So Veach was surprised when Thompson's name was still on the board when the Chiefs were again on the clock 13 picks later.

Thompson, at 5-foot-8 and 200 pounds, is a little undersized, but that doesn't worry Veach.

"He's 5-8, but he's rocked up," Veach said. "He's 200 pounds and looks like he's kind of a bodybuilder with his shirt off. He's got great contact balance. Yards after contact for a small guy, it's really remarkable to see him always keep that ball forward, and he's always finishing runs moving forward. But he's tough, he can do some stuff out of the backfield. I think Coach Reid and the offensive staff are going to have a lot of fun with him."

CHAPTER 16
HOME OF THE CHIEFS

Arrowhead Stadium

Patrick Mahomes, barbecue and a Sea of Red. Does it get any better than this for Chiefs fans on Sundays?

Arrowhead Stadium has been home to the Chiefs for nearly 50 years, and Chiefs fans now hope it is Mahomes' home for years to come. Taking the field for the first time as an NFL starting quarterback at Arrowhead can be a forgettable experience if you're the opposing QB. But if you happened to wear a red No. 15 Chiefs jersey, then it makes for an unforgettable experience.

The first time Mahomes ran through the tunnel as the Chiefs starter came in Week 3 of the 2018 season against the 49ers. Before he took the field, though, he thought he might need to see a doctor.

"My heart was pounding pretty fast," Mahomes said. "It really was an awesome experience. These fans, the passion that they have is unmatched anywhere else in this league. So to be able to run out of the tunnel for the first time—and I was dreaming about it all last year—I'm glad I finally got to do that."

Prior to Mahomes taking over, some said Arrowhead had lost its aura and the home-field advantage the team enjoyed in the 1990s would never return. A string of four-straight heartbreaking playoffs loses in a row at home from 1995 to 2018 can do that, but the Chiefs are bringing the mystique back.

The stadium opened Aug. 12, 1972, when the Chiefs played the St. Louis Cardinals in a preseason game. The Chiefs won 24-14 in front of 78,000 fans. A month later, the Chiefs played the Dolphins in the stadium's first regular-season game and lost 20-10.

The Truman Sports Complex was unlike anything in professional sports as it became the first twin-stadium setup in the country, with then-Royals Stadium—now Kauffman Stadium—opening the following year right across the parking lot.

In 1967, a $100 million bond issue—with $43 million going to the Chiefs and A's for new stadiums that would feature a rolling roof—was brought before Jackson County voters. With Chiefs founder Lamar Hunt and Jack Steadman taking the lead on the project, the bond passed. Shortly after, A's owner Charlie Finley moved the team to Oakland, and Kansas City was left without a baseball team until Ewing Kauffman bought the Royals.

Construction for the stadiums began in 1968 but the rolling roof design was later scrapped due to the project being over budget. Arrowhead cost about $70 million to build, with Hunt contributing millions of his own money.

Kansas City fans cheer on the Chiefs as they take on the San Francisco 49ers on Sept. 23, 2018, at Arrowhead Stadium in Kansas City, Mo. Despite playing in one of the smallest markets the Chiefs have been among the NFL leaders in attendance for years. (Robin Alam/Icon Sportswire)

The stadium was built three stories below ground level, and it is actually narrower than most of today's modern stadiums, which puts Chiefs fans closer to the field. And it's rather vertical structure helps keep noise from getting out.

The Chiefs sold out 155 consecutive games from 1991-2009. The stadium underwent a $375 million renovation in 2010, with the Hunt family contributing $125 million.

"We just decided it was in the best long-range interest of the Chiefs and the Jackson County taxpayers to make the commitment," Clark Hunt said at the time. "We felt that to get it right it was important to go beyond what was required to insure Arrowhead remains one of the greatest stadiums for decades to come."

Despite being one of the smallest markets in the NFL, the Chiefs have consistently been one of the league's best draws. In 2014, Arrowhead became the loudest stadium in the world, setting the Guinness record with a 142.2 decibel roar against the Patriots on Monday Night Football.

"We love it," Chiefs coach Andy Reid said. "There's nothing like Arrowhead when that place is rocking."

The team's lease runs through 2030, and in the coming years, the Chiefs will break ground on one spectacular event while holding out hope another comes to Kansas City. After years of hard work and planning, the NFL announced in May 2019 that Kansas City will host the 2023 NFL Draft.

"Chiefs Kingdom is home to the most passionate fans in the world, and I know they will make Kansas City proud as the host of one of the NFL's premiere events," Hunt said.

And there is still hope that someday Kansas City will host the Super Bowl. So imagine this—Patrick Mahomes, barbecue, a Sea of Red, and the Chiefs playing on Super Bowl Sunday at Arrowhead Stadium. That's the dream for Chiefs fans. Here's hoping it comes true.

ABOUT THE AUTHOR

Jeff Deters is an award-winning journalist and author. He previously covered the Kansas City Chiefs, Kansas City Royals and Kansas Jayhawks for the Topeka Capital-Journal. His work has been honored numerous times by the Kansas Press Association and Kansas City Press Club.

In the early '90s, millions of kids, including Jeff, were glued to their TV sets playing Tecmo Super Bowl. Jeff seems to remember gaining thousands of yards while running over opponents when he was Christian Okoye. He's also pretty certain some of those opponents who flew high into the air and off the screen have defied gravity and not come down yet.

Jeff also recalls flying around the edge as Derrick Thomas and diving full blast into an unsuspecting quarterback countless times. Later, Jeff played football in junior high and high school, became a big fan of Madden games, and started writing books.

Kansas City Chiefs Legends is his second book. His first book, *Miracle Moments in Kansas City Royals History*, was released in July 2017.

Deters lives in Lawrence, Kansas.

BIBLIOGRAPHY

Sources

Much of the information and quotes used in *Kansas City Chiefs Legends* came from the author's coverage of the team and interviews for this book. That included interviews with Eric Berry, Eric Bieniemy, Lloyd Burruss, Harrison Butker, Jamaal Charles, Deron Cherry, Dustin Colquitt, Len Dawson, John Dorsey, Eric Fisher, Dee Ford, Rick Gosselin, Tamba Hali, Tyreek Hill, Justin Houston, Priest Holmes, Mitch Holthus, Clark Hunt, Derrick Johnson, Chris Jones, Travis Kelce, Nick Lowery, Patrick Mahomes, Matt Nagy, Christian Okoye, Andy Reid, Kevin Ross, Mitchell Schwartz, Alex Smith, Emmitt Thomas, Dave Toub, Brett Veach, and more.

Books

Althaus, Bill, *The Good, The Bad and The Ugly*. Triumph Books, 2007.

Flanagan, Jeffery, *Martyball!* Sports Publishing, 2012.

Fulks, Matt, *100 Things Chiefs Fans Should Know and Do Before they Die*. Triumph Books, 2014.

Gretz, Bob, *Hail to the Chiefs*. Singapore Publishing, 1994.

Gretz, Bob, *Tales From the Kansas City Chiefs Sideline*. Sports Publishing, 2015.

MacCambridge, Michael, *Lamar Hunt: A Life in Sports*. Andrews McMeel Publishing, 2012.

McKenzie, Michael, *Arrowhead: Home of the Chiefs*. Taylor Trade Publishing, 1997.

Stallard, Mark, *Kansas City Chiefs Encyclopedia*. Sports Publishing, 2012.

Stram, Hank, with Lou Sahadi, *They're Playing My Game*. Triumph Books, 2006.

Young, Steve, Benedict, Jeff, *QB: My Life Behind the* Spiral. Houghton Mifflin Harcourt, 2016.

Newspapers/Wire Services

Associated Press, Baltimore Sun, Bozeman Daily Chronicle, Charlotte News & Observer, Chicago Tribune, Cleveland Plain Dealer, Dallas Morning News, Houston Chronicle, Kansas City Star, Lawrence Journal-World, Los Angeles Times, Minneapolis Star Tribune, New Orleans Times Picayune, New York Daily News, New York Times, Philadelphia Inquirer, Topeka Capital-Journal, San Francisco Chronicle, Sports Illustrated, USA Today, United Press International, Washington Post.

Websites

Chiefs.com, Deroncherrygolf.com, ESPN.com, Footballmaven.io//talkoffame, FootballPerspective.com, KCUR.org, Lasportshall.com, NFL.com, Mahomes15.com, Nicklowery.com, Profootballhof.com, Profootballreference.com, Seahawks.com, SI.com, 68insidesports.com, Tambatunes.com, Thirdandlong.org, Willtosucceed.org.

www.ingramcontent.com/pod-product-compliance
Lightning Source LLC
Chambersburg PA
CBHW052209090526
44584CB00016BA/1782